Enterprise Data Center
Design and Methodology

Rob Snevely

D1361345

microsystems

Sun Microsystems Press
A Prentice Hall Title

Production Supervision: *Mary Sudul*
Acquisitions Editor: *Eileen Clark*
Editorial Assistant: *Brandt Kenna*
Cover Design Director: *Jerry Votta*
Cover Designer: *Kavish & Kavish Digital Publishing and Design*
Manufacturing Manager: *Alexis R. Heydt*
Marketing Manager: *Debby vanDijk*

Sun Microsystems Press:
Publisher: *Michael Llwyd Alread*

This product is printed digitally on demand.

ISBN 0-13-047393-6

Sun Microsystems Press
A Prentice Hall Title

Acknowledgments

Many thanks to David Yeater of International Consulting Group who took on the herculean challenge of making sure that the jumble of knowledge in my brain actually came out in a form readable by humans. Also thanks to Amr Y. Eissa of International Consulting Group.

To my review team: Elizabeth Purcell, Lisa Elser, Nam Cho, and Adrian Cockcroft, thank you for all your comments, criticisms, and suggestions that made this a better book. I am proud to have worked with all of you, and prouder still to call you all friends.

Special thanks to the Sun BluePrints Technical Publications Manager, Barb Jugo. Without her work and support, this book would never have been published.

Thanks to Gabe Camarillo for his work on the illustrations and photos and ensuring that they all met Sun style guidelines.

Thanks to Julie Snow for all of her effort and help to make sure this book met the required editorial and style guidelines.

Ken Marschall, Rich Carlson, and Gary Beck, a.k.a. "The Management," thanks for all of your support and for having the chutzpeh to back this project, even in tough economic times.

Many thanks to Les Leong and the entire staff of Sun's Enterprise Technology Center in Palo Alto, California, not only for helping me take theoretical ideas and test their effectiveness in the real world, but also for putting up with the cursing and shouting emanating from my office when writers block would strike, as it often did.

Thanks to Scott Bange, John Vanoy Moore, Kristin Fitzgerald, and Debra Maloney-Bolsinger at Jacobs Engineering, and David Pickett, Andy Frichtl, and Dennis Obritschkewitsch at Interface Engineering for their work on the designs for Sun's Enterprise Technology Center in Hillsboro, Oregon.

Thanks to Worldwide Environmental Services, Sun Service, ASHRAE, and NFPA for their work and information provided for the Sun Data Center Site Planning Guide, which was a valuable resource.

I also want to thank the hundreds of Sun customers, system engineers, and sales reps I have been fortunate enough to talk to over the last four years. Your comments and questions about using Sun systems in data centers have provided much "food for thought" on how and why a data center should be designed.

This book is dedicated to four people who have had a profound impact on me.

Scott Holmes: You taught me to believe in myself.

Merle Long: You showed me that you have to be who you are.

Gianni Versace: You made me realize that design is art.

Joey Ramone: You demonstrated the courage that is needed when taking something in a bold new direction.

For everything that you four have given me, I thank you.

This book is dedicated to you guys.

To my two best friends, Allisa Mello and Linda Schneider, thank you so very much for all of your support and encouragement. No one could ever have better friends than you two.

To Marcelline Love, who made the lousiest of days I had writing this book, better. A very heart-felt thank you.

Thanks to Jeff Chen for his support and more importantly, the runs to Del Taco for needed caloric intake.

Thanks to Coca-Cola for Diet Coke and Starbucks Coffee for the venti mocha. Without your caffeine this book would not have been possible. Also thanks to Del Taco for the best fast-food green burritos and hot sauce on the planet.

Finally, thanks must go to Namco for "Soul Caliber," and Activision and Neversoft for "Tony Hawk's Pro Skater 3," two awesome video games which provided some much need distraction.

Contents

Figures

Tables

Preface

"Omne ignotum pro magnifico."

- Tacitus

Designing a data center, whether a new facility or retrofitting an existing one, is no easy, simple task. If you don't interact with people well, if you can't communicate effectively with people who are not in your area of expertise, if you don't enjoy solving difficult problems, if you want a simple, stress-free work life, *don't design a data center*!!!

Okay, now that all the loafing cowards have stopped reading, we can start talking about what this book hopes to accomplish.

This book attempts to walk you through the design process and offers a method that can be used to create a design that meets the requirements of your data center. This book is not a book of designs. It is a tool to work through your requirements and find solutions to create the best design for those requirements.

Early in my career as a system administrator, someone said to me, "Data centers are black magic. They are not understandable or discernible by mere mortals." I can't print my response to that person, but that brief confrontational conversation stuck in my brain. I can tell you, designing data centers isn't "black magic." A data center is a complex and interdependent environment, however, it can be broken down into smaller, more manageable pieces. Methodologies can be used that make designing data centers understandable and discernible by mere mortals. To that person many years ago who tried to tell me otherwise, I have this to say: "You were wrong, and this book proves it!"

Over the years, I've worked in a number of different data centers, and in that time I've had the opportunity to talk to many of Sun's customers about their centers and take tours through them. What I repeatedly found, with very few exceptions, was that there was no overall design methodology used when planning these centers. If there was a methodology, it usually came out of overcoming one or two problems that had bitten these people in previous data centers. Sometimes the problem areas were so over-designed that it forced other design areas to suffer.

Often, the people who designed the space had never worked in data center environments. They typically designed commercial spaces like offices and warehouses and they used one basic method or formula for the design criteria: *watts per square foot*. This method assumes that the equipment load across the entire space is uniform. In every data center I have seen, the equipment load has never been uniform. Add to this that all of the pieces that make up a data center (power, cooling, floor load, connectivity, etc.) are all interrelated and dependent on each other. It became very clear that this old method of watts per square foot was not an effective or efficient design method. A better method that could address these issues was needed.

When I started trying to create this new design methodology, I looked to other sources of design for information and inspiration, what Shakespeare would have probably referred to as muses. These run the gamut from classical antiquity to modern pop culture, and from artists and philosophers to fashion designers and punk rock musicians. At the beginning of every chapter in this book is a quote from one of these many muses. I hope that they can help provide you with similar inspiration, or better still, help you find your own muses.

So, just what does "Omne ignotum, pro magnifico" mean? It translates as "Everything unknown is taken for magnificent." It means "Everything is commonplace by explanation." With information, reason, inspiration, and hard work, many things, including designing a data center, are understandable and doable.

So let's get started! Or, to borrow a phrase from my Southern California Skateboarder's Lexicon, "Let's get radical!"

Sun BluePrints Program

The mission of the Sun BluePrints Program is to empower Sun's customers with the technical knowledge required to implement reliable, extensible, and secure information systems within the datacenter using Sun products. This program provides a framework to identify, develop, and distribute best practices information that applies across the Sun product lines. Experts in technical subjects in various areas contribute to the program and focus on the scope and usefulness of the information.

The Sun BluePrints Program includes books, guides, and online articles. Through these vehicles, Sun can provide guidance, installation and implementation experiences, real-life scenarios, and late-breaking technical information.

The monthly electronic magazine, Sun BluePrints OnLine, is located on the Web at http://www.sun.com/blueprints. To be notified about updates to the Sun BluePrints Program, please register yourself on this site.

Who Should Use This Book

This book is primarily intended for readers with varying degrees of experience or knowledge of data center technology. It is written for System and Network Administrators, MIS/IT managers, Operations staff, and Information Technology executives who would like a complete overview of the data center design process.

Before You Read This Book

You should be familiar with the basic administration and maintenance functions of a data center.

How This Book Is Organized

This book contains the following chapters and appendixes.

Chapter 1, "Data Center Design Philosophy," presents the author's philosophy of designing a data center sanely and efficiently, including the top ten guidelines.

Chapter 2, "Data Center Design Criteria," discusses the primary criteria of data center design including project scope, budget, availability profiles, insurance, building code, and determining the viability of the project.

Chapter 3, "Designing a Data Center," discusses the basic design process, the key players, the method of designing for data center capacities, determining the structural layout and support systems, networking, redundancy, security, monitoring, and system health.

Chapter 4, "Determining Data Center Capacities," could be considered the heart of the book. It describes the use of rack location units (RLUs) to determine the best design for the data center. It bases the design on the data center and equipment capacities rather than on electrical needs and square footage. It will take you through the planning stages and explain how to create RLU definitions in the early design stages.

Chapter 5, "Site Selection," examines locating the data center in either an existing location or a build-to-suit situation. It takes an in-depth look at budget, access, security, capacity, environmental restrictions, and numerous other details to consider in selecting the best location.

Chapter 6, "Implementing a Raised Floor," describes the several purposes of a raised floor system, the benefits of using this system over other systems, and goes into important structural details such as the support grid, tile construction, and load capabilities. It also covers the use of the subfloor space for air flow and cable routing.

Chapter 7, "Power Distribution," examines all aspects of the data center's power requirements and support systems. It covers assessing power needs, safety, redundancy, backup power systems, grounding and bonding, the signal reference grid, wiring and cabling, power quality, avoiding electromagnetic and electrostatic problems, and the optional use of power distribution units.

Chapter 8, "HVAC and Other Environmental Controls," takes you through the entire data center air flow and cooling system from HVAC units to the external support systems. It discusses the problems inherent in cooling a data center and how to remedy them. Other aspects are described, such as humidification, temperature and RH monitoring, mechanical support systems, proper air flow, exchange, pressure, and quality, and efficient placement of equipment.

Chapter 9, "Network Cabling Infrastructure," describes various devices and cabling scenarios for the data center network. It discusses the structure of the network, network hierarchy and modular design, connectivity between equipment and to the ISP, proper routing, cable identification, and verification.

Chapter 10, "Shipping, Receiving, and Staging," describes important but often overlooked aspects of the data center that should be considered in the initial design phases. Heavy equipment must be moved in and out of the center and it must go through packing, unpacking, and setup procedures. This chapter covers aspects of the loading dock, staging area, and storage areas.

Chapter 11, "Avoiding Hazards," discusses the gamut of natural and man-made hazards including fire, earthquake, flooding, and noise. It also discusses human safety and avoiding unauthorized access.

Chapter 12, "Environmental Contaminants," describes many of the contaminants that can cause operator health problems and compromise the operations of data center equipment. The different types of contaminants are discussed, how they can adversely affect operations, and how to avoid them. Solutions include positive pressurization and quality filtration.

Chapter 13, "Codes and Construction," discusses the convoluted topic of codes and their many incarnations, and gives some basic construction criteria.

Appendix A, "Managing System Configurations," A reprint of the October 2001 SuperG paper by Elizabeth Purcell. This paper examines the challanges of accurate system configuration managment including configuration management for software revisions, network interfaces, storage subsystems, firmware, and patches.

Appendix B, "Bibliography and References," lists books, other technical documentation, organizations, and software.

The Glossary is a list of terms and acronyms used frequently in the course of discussing data centers.

Ordering Sun Documents

The SunDocs℠ program provides more than 250 manuals from Sun Microsystems, Inc. If you live in the United States, Canada, Europe, or Japan, you can purchase documentation sets or individual manuals through this program.

Accessing Sun Documentation Online

The docs.sun.com Web site enables you to access Sun technical documentation online. You can browse the docs.sun.com archive or search for a specific book title or subject. The URL is http://docs.sun.com/.

Typographic Conventions

The following table describes the typographic changes used in this book.

Typeface or Symbol	Meaning	Example
AaBbCc123	The names of commands, files, and directories; on-screen computer output	Edit your `.login` file. Use `ls -a` to list all files. `machine_name% You have mail.`
AaBbCc123	What you type, contrasted with on-screen computer output	`machine_name%` **su** `Password:`
AaBbCc123	Command-line placeholder: replace with a real name or value	To delete a file, type `rm` *filename*.
AaBbCc123	Book titles, new words or terms, or words to be emphasized	Read Chapter 6 in *User's Guide*. These are called *class* options. You *must* be root to do this.

Shell Prompts in Command Examples

The following table shows the default system prompt and superuser prompt for the C shell, Bourne shell, and Korn shell.

Shell	Prompt
C shell prompt	`machine_name%`
C shell superuser prompt	`machine_name#`
Bourne shell and Korn shell prompt	`$`
Bourne shell and Korn shell superuser prompt	`#`

CHAPTER 1

Data Center Design Philosophy

"Form follows function."

  - Louis Henri Sullivan

The detailed process of data center design appears on the outset to be a purely mechanical process involving the layout of the area, computations to determine equipment capacities, and innumerable other engineering details. They are, of course, essential to the design and creation of a data center, however, the mechanics alone do not a data center make. The use of pure mechanics rarely creates anything that is useful, except perhaps by chance.

There are, in fact, some philosophical guidelines that should be kept in mind during the data center design process. These are based on the relatively short history of designing and building practical data centers, but are also based on design concepts going way back. This chapter looks at some of these philosophies.

This chapter contains the following sections:

- "Look Forward by Looking Back"
- "A Modern Pantheon"
- "Fundamentals of the Philosophy"
- "Top Ten Data Center Design Guidelines"

Look Forward by Looking Back

The idea that technology is relatively new, that it arose within the last fifty to one hundred years, is a common misconception. There have been great advances, particularly in the electronic age, but the truth of the matter is that technology has been around since human beings began bashing rock against rock.

One of the most interesting things about design is that it draws from many sources. Paintings by Raphael and Botticelli in the Renaissance were dependent on the mathematics of perspective geometry developed more than a millennia and a half before either were born. They also drew on the language and form of classical architecture and Greco-Roman mythology to provide settings for many of their works. Raphael and Botticelli created works that had never been seen before, but they could not have done this without the groundwork that had been set down in the previous centuries.

Look back to the most prolific designers and engineers in the history of western civilization: The Romans. Roman advances in design and technology are still with us today. If you cross a bridge to get to work, or take the subway, or walk down the street to get a latte, chances are you are doing so using elements of Roman design and technology. These elements are the arch and concrete.

When entering the Pantheon in Rome, most people probably don't remark, "What a great use of the arch!" and "That dome is a single concrete structure." However, without the modular design of the arch and the invention of concrete, the Roman Pantheon could not have been built.

The Romans understood that the arch, by design, had strength and the ability to transfer load from its center down to its base. They had used the arch in modular and linear ways to build bridges and carry water for their water systems. But in the Pantheon, the modularity of the arch realized its true potential. Spin an arch at its center point and you create a dome. This means that across any point in the span you have the strength of the arch. Also, they had found that concrete could be used to bond all of these arches together as a single dome. Concrete allowed this dome structure to scale beyond any other dome of its time. It would take eighteen centuries for technology to advance to the point where a larger dome than that of the Pantheon could be built.

What does the architecture of ancient Rome have to do with data centers? The physical architecture itself has little in common with data centers, but the design philosophy of this architecture does. In both cases, new ideas on how to construct things were needed. In both cases, using the existing design philosophies of the time, "post and lintel" for ancient Rome, and "watts per square foot" for data centers, would not scale to new requirements. It is this idea, the design philosophy of modular, scalable units, that is critical to meet the requirements of today's data centers and, more importantly, the data centers of the future.

A Modern Pantheon

A modern data center still shares many aspects with ancient architecture, structurally and in service. The form literally follows the function. The purpose of both the Pantheon and a data center is to provide services. To provide services, its requirements for continual functioning must be met. This is the design team's primary concern. The design of the data center must revolve around the care and feeding of the service providing equipment.

These functional requirements of the data center are:

- A place to locate computer, storage, and networking devices safely and securely
- To provide the power needed to maintain these devices
- To provide a temperature-controlled environment within the parameters needed to run these devices
- To provide connectivity to other devices both inside and outside the data center

In the design philosophy of this book, these needs must be met and in the most efficient way possible. The efficiency of the data center system relies entirely on the efficiency of the design. The fundamental principles of a data center philosophy should be your guiding principles.

The phrase "design philosophy" could have many different meanings. For the purposes of this book we'll use the following definition: A design philosophy is the application of structure to the functional requirements of an object based on a reasoned set of values.

Fundamentals of the Philosophy

There are five core values that are the foundation of a data center design philosophy: simplicity, flexibility, scalability, modularity, and sanity. The last one might give you pause, but if you've had previous experience in designing data centers, it makes perfect sense.

Design decisions should always be made with consideration to these values.

Keep the Design as Simple as Possible

A simple data center design is easier to understand and manage. A basic design makes it simple to do the best work and more difficult to do sloppy work. For example, if you label everything—network ports, power outlets, cables, circuit breakers, their location on the floor—there is no guess work involved. When people set up a machine, they gain the advantage of knowing ahead of time where the machine goes and where everything on that machine should be plugged in. It is also simpler to verify that the work was done correctly. Since the locations of all of the connections to the machine are pre-labeled and documented, it is simple to record the information for later use, should the machine develop a problem.

FIGURE 1-1 Simple, Clean, Modular Data Center Equipment Room

Design for Flexibility

Nobody knows where technology will be in five years, but it is a good guess that there will be some major changes. Making sure that the design is flexible and easily upgradable is critical to a successful long-term design.

Part of flexibility is making the design cost-effective. Every design decision has an impact on the budget. Designing a cost effective data center is greatly dependent on the mission of the center. One company might be planning a data center for mission critical applications, another for testing large-scale configurations that will go into a mission critical data center. For the first company, full backup generators to drive the entire electrical load of the data center might be a cost-effective solution. For the second company, a UPS with a 20-minute battery life might be sufficient. Why the difference? If the data center in the first case goes down, it could cost the company two million dollars a minute. Spending five million on full backup generators would be worth the expense to offset the cost of downtime. In the second case, the cost of down time might be $10,000 an hour. It would take 500 hours of unplanned downtime to recoup the initial cost of five million dollars of backup generators.

Design for Scalability

The design should work equally well for a 2,000, 20,000, or 2,000,000 square foot data center. Where a variety of equipment is concerned, the use of watts per square foot to design a data center does not scale because the needs of individual machines are not taken into consideration. This book describes the use of rack location units (RLUs) to design for equipment needs. This system is scalable and can be reverse-engineered.

Use a Modular Design

Data centers are highly complex things, and complex things can quickly become unmanageable. Modular design allows you to create highly complex systems from smaller, more manageable building blocks.

These smaller units are more easily defined and can be more easily replicated. They can also be defined by even smaller units, and you can take this to whatever level of granularity necessary to manage the design process. The use of this type of hierarchy has been present in design since antiquity.

Keep Your Sanity

Designing and building a data center can be very stressful. There are many things that can, and will, go wrong. Keep your sense of humor. Find ways to enjoy what you're doing. Using the other four values to evaluate design decisions should make the process easier as they give form, order, and ways to measure the value and sense of the design decisions you're making. Primarily, they help to eliminate as many unknowns as possible, and eliminating the unknowns will make the process much less stressful.

Top Ten Data Center Design Guidelines

The following are the top ten guidelines selected from a great many other guidelines, many of which are described throughout this book.

1. **Plan ahead.** You never want to hear "Oops!" in your data center.

2. **Keep it simple.** Simple designs are easier to support, administer, and use. Set things up so that when a problem occurs, you can fix it quickly.

3. **Be flexible.** Technology changes. Upgrades happen.

4. **Think modular.** Look for modularity as you design. This will help keep things simple and flexible.

5. **Use RLUs, not square feet.** Move away from the concept of using square footage of area to determine capacity. Use RLUs to define capacity and make the data center scalable.

6. **Worry about weight.** Servers and storage equipment for data centers are getting denser and heavier every day. Make sure the load rating for all supporting structures, particularly for raised floors and ramps, is adequate for current and future loads.

7. **Use aluminum tiles in the raised floor system.** Cast aluminum tiles are strong and will handle increasing weight load requirements better than tiles made of other materials. Even the perforated and grated aluminum tiles maintain their strength and allow the passage of cold air to the machines.

8. **Label everything.** Particularly cabling! It is easy to let this one slip when it seems as if "there are better things to do." The time lost in labeling is time gained when you don't have to pull up the raised floor system to trace the end of a single cable. And you *will* have to trace bad cables!

9. **Keep things covered, or bundled, and out of sight.** If it can't be seen, it can't be messed with.

10. **Hope for the best, plan for the worst.** That way, you're never surprised.

CHAPTER 2

Data Center Design Criteria

"It is an old maxim of mine that when you have excluded the impossible, whatever remains, however improbable, must be the truth."

- Sherlock Holmes, by Sir Arthur Conan Doyle

The criteria for a data center are the requirements that must be met to provide the system capacities and availability necessary to run the business. Due to the special circumstances of each facility, it would be difficult to give a comprehensive list of all criteria involved in data center design. The possibilities are vast, and it isn't the intention of this book to give a definitive set of design plans to follow, but rather to guide you toward your final design by listing and describing the most probable criteria. The goal of this chapter is to arm you with the knowledge you need to begin the design process.

This chapter contains the following sections:

- "Scope, Budget, and Criteria"
- "System Availability Profiles"
- "Insurance and Local Building Codes"
- "Determining the Viability of the Project"

Scope, Budget, and Criteria

An important distinction to make at this point is what really constitutes the elements of a data center. When we talk about the data center, we are talking about the site, the Command Center (if one is to be added), the raised floor (if one is to be added), the network infrastructure (switches, routers, terminal servers, and support equipment providing the core logical infrastructure), the environmental controls, and power. Though a data center contains servers and storage system components (usually contained in racks), these devices are contents of the data center, not part of the data center. They are transient contents just as DVDs might be considered the transient contents of a DVD player. The data center is more of a permanent fixture, while the servers and storage systems are movable, adaptable, interchangeable elements. However, just as the DVD is of no value without the player and the player is of no value without the DVD, a data center without equipment is an expensive empty room, and servers with no connection are just expensive paper weights. The design of the data center must include all of the elements. The essential elements are called the criteria.

Project Scope

Most often, it is the project scope that determines the data center design. The scope must be determined based on the company's data center needs (the desired or required capacities of the system and network infrastructure), as well as the amount of money available. The scope of the project could be anything from constructing a separate building in another state with offices and all the necessary utilities, to simply a few server and storage devices added to an existing data center. In either case, those creating the project specifications should be working closely with those responsible for the budget.

Budget

Designing a data center isn't just about what the company needs or wants, it's what they're willing to pay for.

Using project scope as a starting point, the criteria for the data center can be loosely determined, and a comparison between how much this will cost and the budget will determine the viability of the project. Is there too much money or too little? (Okay, in theory you could get more money for the data center than you need, but this rarely happens.) Then the balancing act begins. If there isn't enough money in the budget to cover the cost of essential elements, either more money must be allocated, or some creative modifications must be made to the project scope.

The process for determining a budget, deciding what parts of the data center will receive what portion of it, and putting together a center based on designated funds is one of negotiation, trade-offs, compromises, and creativity. Also, there is probably more than one budget for the data center, and how the money is allocated depends on numerous factors specific to the company.

Planning a data center is part of larger business considerations, and both designers and those setting the budget must be flexible. Accountants telling the data center designers, "Here's how much you get. Make a data center," probably won't work. By the same token, designers demanding enough money for the ideal data center probably won't meet with approval by the accountants. When negotiating for funds, the best idea is to have several alternative plans.

Some questions and considerations that must be examined in the beginning might include:

- What is the budget for the data center?
- Are the project scope and the budget a realistic balance?
- Is there enough money to create an adequate center for the company's needs?
- How much do you actually need to create the center?
- How will funds be distributed? Can funds be redistributed?
- Factor in running costs, servicing, and maintenance contracts with maintenance suppliers.
- Factor in redundancy of power/services/HVAC/UPS.
- Consider carefully all possible future modifications, upgrades, changes in power needs, and system additions in the design.

The toughest thing about designing a data center is working within the budget. The budget will force you to make compromises and you must figure out whether or not you are making the right compromises. You might be able to cut costs by removing the backup generators from the budget, but you must weigh the risk of such a decision. There is the possibility that the data center power might fail and systems would be out of action without backup power. Every compromise carries a degree of risk. Do the risks outweigh the cost? Figuring out how to meet the budget is where your finance people and risk analysts really come into play. Use their expertise. Here are a few questions you might work out with your finance and risk team.

- If cost exceeds budget, can anything be removed or replaced with a less expensive alternative?
- Are all redundant systems really necessary?
- How much will projected failures (downtime) cost compared to initial costs for redundant systems?
- Is a separate Command Center necessary?
- Can amortization schedules be stretched from, for example, three years to five years so there is money available for other needs?
- Can certain areas be expanded or upgraded later?
- What is the best time to bring the facility online? In the U.S., amortization doesn't begin until you occupy the space. Would it be better to take the amortization *hit* this fiscal year or the next?

A final point to consider: As with many aspects of data center design, the money spent on planning is invariably money well spent. It costs money to build a data center, and part of that expenditure comes right up front in coming up with a budget. Money spent on creating an accurate budget can actually save money in the long run.

Build Budget and Run Budget

The build budget is the money allocated to build and bring up the data center. The previous three sections describe what is covered by the build budget (or budgets, if separate). But you must also consider the run budget which is the amount of money allocated for yearly operating costs, maintenance, repair, ISP network connectivity, service and support agreements on computers, storage and network equipment, and the cost of electricity. These should be considered as part of the run budget.

Criteria

The most important criteria for a data center can be put into the following categories:

- Location (or site)
- Essential criteria
- Secondary criteria

Location

It would seem that the site you choose for your data center would be considered one of the essential criteria. It's true that where you choose to locate the data center site (region/building) is important, but this choice is based on many different factors. For example, a company wants to build a new data center near their corporate offices in Cleveland, Ohio. To meet project scope on the essential criteria, it is determined that several million dollars more are needed, just to secure the site location. Suddenly, building in Cleveland doesn't seem as critical if a few million dollars can be saved by locating the building one hundred and sixty miles away in Milford Center where land prices are much cheaper.

Also, connectivity through the company's network infrastructure has made it possible for a data center to be located wherever it is practical and affordable. A data center can even use multiple locations, if necessary, connecting through the network. In this way, location is a very flexible and negotiable criteria.

Essential Criteria

There is a hierarchy of essential criteria. All data centers must have the following four elements in whatever capacities are needed or available. Though they are listed in order of importance, a data center cannot run without all of them working interdependently. It is only their values that are negotiable.

- **Physical capacity.** You must have space and weight capacity for equipment, and therefore, the other three criteria. There must be space for the equipment and the floor must be able to support the weight. This is a constant.

- **Power.** Without power nothing can run. Power is either on or off. Connections to different parts of the grid and/or utilizing a UPS increases uptime. You must have physical capacity to have room for power and the equipment that needs power.

- **Cooling.** Without cooling nothing will run for long. This is either on or off, though redundancy increases uptime. You must have physical capacity and power to run HVACs.

- **Bandwidth.** Without connectivity, the data center is of little value. The type and amount of bandwidth is device dependent. You must have physical capacity, power, and cooling to even consider connectivity.

Unless the data center will be used for non-mission-critical operations, the last three criteria should be designed to be up and running 100 percent of the time.

The use of these elements is non-negotiable, but their values are negotiable. Consider a decision about power redundancy. A UPS system (batteries that kick in when the power goes out) is less expensive than creating a power generation plant, but it has a limited run time. For a mission-critical operation, the 20 minutes of power a UPS might give you could be insufficient.

Let's say the UPS costs $1 million, and the power generation plant costs $3.5 million. The track record of the power company shows that they're down an average of 15-minutes once a year. For your company, a 15-minute power outage equals two hours for the outage and recovery time. Two hours of downtime costs the company $500,000. With a UPS system, there would be no outage because the 20 minutes afforded by the batteries would easily cover for the 15 minute outage and there would be no recovery time needed. Therefore, it would take two years to recover the $1 million dollar cost of the UPS, whereas it would take seven years to recover the cost of the power generation plant. If the power company has a greater problem with power outages, the generators make sense. Or relocating to an area with more dependable power might make more sense.

Secondary Criteria

The essential criteria must be included in the design in whatever values are available. However, there are invariably other criteria that must be considered, but they are secondary. The level of importance of secondary criteria is wholly dependent on the company and project scope. It's conceivable that the budget could be trimmed, for example, in fixtures, but it's likely that you'll want to budget in overhead lighting so data center personnel won't have to work with flashlights held between their teeth. Still, you can see that some criteria is very flexible.

Examples of secondary criteria are:

- Fixtures such as plumbing and lighting
- Walls, doors, windows, offices, loading dock
- All of the miscellaneous hardware, security cameras, card readers, door knobs, equipment cabinets, etc.
- Equipment such as forklifts and pallet jacks
- A Command Center

These will vary depending on whether you're building a new structure or retrofitting an old one, but what is key is the negotiating value of these elements.

The equation for the total budget is:

essential criteria + secondary criteria + location = budget

or

budget = essential criteria + secondary criteria + location

Using Rack Location Units

A concept that will help the data center designer considerably in determining the essential criteria (how much equipment can the center support and what capacities are necessary to support the equipment) is that of rack location units (RLUs). These are numbers based on the operating requirements of each rack in the data center. A rack could be considered to have specific RLU values based on its essential requirements (power, cooling, etc.) and these numbers could be used in relation to other devices with the same, or similar, requirements. In a data center with varied equipment, more than one RLU definition is usually required. For example, all of the storage racks in one section of the data center might be considered to be all RLU-A racks, and all the server racks might be considered RLU-B racks.

This is a very important design concept to understand and is covered in greater detail in Chapter 4, "Determining Data Center Capacities."

System Availability Profiles

Companies with lower access considerations (businesses that aren't open all hours, such as retail chain stores) might have fewer availability requirements than, for example, businesses that do national banking, government agencies, and the health care industry. The availability needs of the data center equipment should be determined in the project scope. Knowing which devices, or groups of devices, are mission-critical (needed 24×7×365) and which devices are in any availability level below mission-critical is important in determining many aspects of data center design, primarily system redundancies. These include:

- **Device redundancies.** The number of backup devices that must be available in the event of equipment failures.

- **Power redundancies.** The number of feeds from different parts of the grid, the number of UPS systems, etc., that must be installed to make sure these systems stay running.

- **Cooling redundancies.** The number of extra HVAC units that must be available in the event that one or more units fail.

- **Network redundancies.** The amount of network equipment that must be available in the event of failure. The number of connections to your ISP. The number of network feeds needed to multiple ISPs in the event that one has a catastrophic failure.

In most situations, a data center won't have a single availability profile. Several jobs could be going on from machine to machine, and some tasks have greater availability levels than others, some highly critical. Some might need to be highly available, but are less critical. Determining risk of all the operations is key to making many design decisions.

Consider the following example. The Chekhovian Bank of Molière decides to upgrade their computer systems and install a data center to keep up with their massive transaction needs. When deciding how to outfit the data center, the question of how available the equipment must be comes up. There are several operations of the data center and they all have different availability profiles. Historical data of the company's operations and general trends help to determine the availability profile of their machines.

The following graph shows the Chekhovian Bank's projected availability profile.

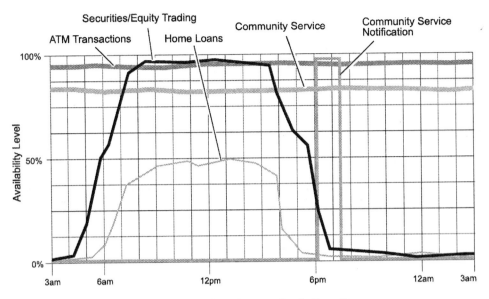

FIGURE 2-1   Availability Profile of the Chekhovian Bank Data Center

Here is an analysis of the this profile:

- ATM transactions which are highly utilized (mission-critical) must be available around the clock. Redundant systems are essential.

- Security and equities trading must be constantly available during business hours (mission-critical) and moderately available the remaining parts of the day. Redundant systems are essential.

- Home loans are important but some occasional downtime won't be disastrous. Redundancy is a good idea, though this is where corners can be cut.

- The Community Services Web site should be up and running around-the-clock so people can access the information, but this is a non-critical service and some downtime won't hurt. Redundancy is probably not worthwhile.

- The Community Services email mailers are sent only once a week in the evening and, though important, it won't hurt the company if the mailers go out late on occasion. No redundancy is required.

Risk-assessment analysts are hired to look at each part of the profile to determine the cost of downtime in each area and help decide the best course of action. They determine that the servers for ATM transactions and equity trading are mission-critical. The cost of either department going down will cost the bank $500,000 per minute of down time. Using the RLU model, the data center designer can calculate that these systems require 200kW of electricity. The cost of a 200kW generator is $2 million. The cost of a 20-minute UPS for 200kW is $450,000. So, for $2.45 million the bank can provide power to its configurations. Since all it would take is a 5-minute outage to lose $2.5 million, a generator and a UPS are considered a viable expenditure.

The servers for the Home Loan portion of the bank require 100kW of power and the risk analysts determine that an outage to this department will cost $5,000 per minute. The cost of a 100kW generator would cost $1 million. A 20 minute UPS for 100kW would be $300,000. The risk analysts also went to the Artaudian Power & Electric Company and got historical information on power outages in the area during the last five years. This data shows that they will average 2 outages a year, but the duration of these outages will be less than ten minutes. Also, the ATM and equity trading groups need a 200kW 20-minute UPS. This UPS can be upgraded to a 300kW twenty minute UPS for only $150,000. At two 10-minute outages a year, the cost of this UPS upgrade will pay for itself in a year and a half. This upgrade is deemed viable but the 100kW generator is not, because it would take 200 minutes of outages of more than 20 minutes to recoup the expenditure.

The systems that run the Community Services web site and mailers represent no significant loss of revenue for the bank if they are down for even a few days. It is determined that no additional cost for increased availability will be approved for these systems.

The cost of services to increase availability is a continuum. Each step in increasing availability has a cost. At some point, the cost of the next step might not be worth the amount of system downtime. So, determining what the availability profile of a configuration will be is determined by the cost of having this configuration unavailable. As mentioned at the beginning of the "Budget" section, it is not about providing your customers with what they want. They always want it all. It's about how much money they are willing to spend to get what they want. It's a cost-effective trade-off.

Insurance and Local Building Codes

Insurance and local building codes will have an effect on many design decisions and should be considered in every aspect of the design process by the entire design team, including all building contractors. The contractors on the team will probably be aware of the constraints and specifications of the insurance carrier and local building codes, but the insurers and building authorities must approve the final plans.

In the U.S., you need code approval twice; first for the building plans, then, after the construction is complete. The later approval ensures that everything was installed according to code as it was documented in the approved plans.

It is important for everyone working on the project to be aware of these constraints to avoid unnecessary changes to the plans at the last minute. The best assurance of time well spent is to have a continual dialog with insurers and building authorities during the design phases.

Codes are covered in greater detail in Chapter 13, "Codes and Construction."

Determining the Viability of the Project

There are times when too many compromises must be made to make the data center project viable. It might be something obvious (you can't get enough power from the local power company or there are frequent flooding problems), or it might be a number of small factors that, when looked at collectively, show that the project is a bad risk. Consider the following possible constraints on the project:

- Inadequate budget
- Retrofit problems such as grounding, cable routing, inadequate floor to ceiling height, no way to set up seismic restraints, etc.
- Better business decision to use co-location or ISP, if only temporarily
- Inadequate pool of qualified employees
- Overly expensive location
- Inadequate district or too remote
- Inadequate or inappropriate space
- Inadequate power. Can't connect to separate parts of the grid for redundancy
- Inadequate cooling capacity
- Inadequate ISP service
- Local building codes, insurance, or fire regulations are too restrictive
- Too many weather or seismic problems
- High history of fires

Most of these problems have to do with the inadequacies of the location. For more information, see Chapter 5, "Site Selection."

CHAPTER 3

Designing a Data Center

"It is a capital mistake to theorize before one has data."

- Sherlock Holmes, by Sir Arthur Conan Doyle

This chapter describes the most important design decisions that must be made in planning a data center. A few of the topics are described in more detail in later chapters.

This chapter contains the following sections:

- "Design Process"
- "Data Center Structural Layout"
- "Data Center Support Systems"
- "Physical and Logical Security"
- "System Monitoring"
- "Remote Systems Management"
- "Planning for Possible Expansion"

Design Process

The design stages for the data center usually take the skills of architects, accountants, structural, mechanical, electrical, HVAC, system, and network engineers, project managers, and procurement personnel. Add also the probability of sales personnel, insurance carriers, and risk management analysts. Overseeing the project is a data center design engineer whose task is to accommodate the requirements of the system and network engineers, and to work with the other members of the team to ensure that the data center requirements (based on the project scope) are met.

As in any other design process, this is an iterative and recursive process. You have an initial set of criteria and you use this set of criteria to determine requirements. You define rack location units (RLUs, described in Chapter 4, "Determining Data Center Capacities") to ensure that the requirements match or exceed the criteria. At certain points other criteria will emerge. These, in turn, change the requirements. And additional or different RLUs will be needed to verify these requirements meet or exceed this new criteria. This is how the process is iterative. Other times, requirements change, and this changes the criteria which in turn changes the requirements. This is how the process is recursive. After several passes through this iterative recursion, a stable set of criteria and requirements will emerge. The changes become smaller in scope, and the process continues as before, albeit with a finer level of granularity.

Just when you think you have a handle on the whole design, somebody tries to get code approval for something, won't get it, and you end up very close to square one. You then have a great screaming match with a white board marker because you're convinced it picked that exact moment to dry up on you. You're certain that its reason for doing this was just to annoy you (the fact that you left the cap off for three days is irrelevant). Finally, you decide to see how far you can throw it across the parking lot.

Then, you and a few friends head off to the pub for a few pints. You become more rational and realize, "Oh, it's not that bad... We can just add another network POD in this other row and that will fix the problem, and I can figure that out tomorrow morning in fifteen minutes." Things get back to only mild insanity for a few days until a similar event triggers similar behavior. Over time, the problems get smaller and eventually the design meets the criteria.

While the description of events above might seem a little over the top (you usually end up throwing your dead white board marker across your office rather than the parking lot), it is not that far from the truth. If you are embarking on designing and building a data center, remember this above all else: Find ways to have fun, enjoy the process, and learn to see the humor in some of the bizarre situations you'll find yourself in. If you don't, you might as well get a long-term lease on a padded cell and start your fittings for a jacket with sleeves that tie behind the neck.

Design Drawings

It should be kept in mind that the design of a data center should be structured but fluid, not only during the design process, but after construction. Computer environments constantly evolve to accommodate company needs, changes in technology, and the business landscape. Professional, detailed plans are necessary in the design stages, but it is important to keep updated working drawings of the data center and all support systems.

Computer Aided Design (CAD) software is typically used. It is more efficient than drawing by hand, and creates plans that are clearly readable, easily reproduced, and easily modified. These blueprints allow for the continued updating of architectural, electrical, mechanical, and computer systems. The drawings can be used in site evaluations and future planning.

Blueprints are particularly important when the project involves outside contractors. Some of the primary contractors are:

- **Architectural firms.** They might supply actual drawings of the building, showing a wall here, door there, lobby over there, where carpet will be installed, where concrete will be used. This represents the physical building.

- **Interior designers.** They create the "look" of the place, sometimes matching company specifications for consistency of styles, from trim to carpet.

- **Structural engineers.** They make sure the building will use materials and construction techniques that will keep the roof from collapsing under the weight of all those cooling towers.

- **Electrical design firms and engineers.** They deal with lighting plans, electrical distribution, wireways under the floor, breaker subpanels, power transformers, wiring for the fire detection system, and smoke alarms.

- **HVAC design firms.** They determine HVAC unit placement and whether they should be 20-ton or 30-ton, determine proper installation of piping that brings chilled fluids to units, and where cooling towers, compressors, and heat exchangers will be located.

Some of these tasks, such as electrical and HVAC, might be handled by the same firm. It could depend on who is available in the area. It is a good idea to employ a project management firm to coordinate all of these different contractors.

FIGURE 3-1 Large Scale Design Drawings from the General Contractor or the Project Management Company

Thanks to the Internet, you can access the drawings electronically (Adobe® PDF format works well for this). This can reduce the time of the design/review/change process considerably. The CAD drawings are usually held by the building contractor who helps coordinate all the other subcontractors. PDFs are good, but, a few times in the cycle, you will need actual blueprints which are larger in scale than most computer monitors. These allow you to see very fine details that might be lost in a PDF file. Also, they provide a place to make notes directly on the drawings for later use.

During the design process, you should also have several dozen pads of Post-It Notes for temporary comments on the blueprints and to bring certain details to the attention of others. You should also have a large white board with lots of dry erase markers in a variety of colors. (Remember to put the caps back on the markers when not in use.)

Designing for Data Center Capacities

A major problem in designing a data center is determining how to support equipment of known quantity and capacities, or determining the quantities of equipment of unknown capacities for a data center of known capacities. In other words, how do you make the equipment fit the room, or how do you make the room fit the equipment? There are many factors to consider and often these factors are limitations. Looking at the problem from the point of view of capacities is helpful, but you can also think of these as limitations, which is usually the case. The room might only be so big and the power company might only be able to give you so much electricity. Some of the major limitations are:

- Budget
- District
- Insurance and building code
- Power
- Cooling
- Connectivity
- Site
- Space
- Weight

A delicate balancing act must occur between many of the members of the design and build team to determine the capacities and limitation,, and to work with them. With this knowledge, factors can be juggled to decide how to implement what is available to meet the project scope. If the limitations are too great, the project scope must change.

This book offers a useful (some might say essential) tool for designing based on data center capacities called RLU. This is discussed in greater detail in Chapter 4, "Determining Data Center Capacities."

Data Center Structural Layout

The data center must be designed to accommodate diverse hardware designs and requirements, and possibly equipment from different manufacturers. Determining RLUs is the best way to decide how the space will be filled with equipment, and with this information, where the equipment will be placed. The following general guidelines should be used in planning the initial layout of the room, keeping future planning in mind.

Note – Though the plans for the data center do not include the storage and server equipment it will contain, it is necessary to know what the equipment will be to make many of the design decisions for the data center.

Structural Considerations

There are any number of structural issues to consider when designing a data center. Here is a sampling of some actual issues you might face:

- **Building in an area with a subfloor to ceiling height of ten feet.** By the time you add two feet for the raised floor, the height is reduced to eight feet. Now add the twelve inches needed for light fixtures and fire suppression systems, and your space is reduced to seven feet. The racks that will occupy this space are seven feet tall and exhaust heat out the top, or rather, they would if there was room. These racks will overheat *real fast*. This is not a realistic space in which to build a data center.

- **Building in the basement of a building that overlooks a river.** After construction is complete, you find out that the river overflows its banks every few years and you don't have any pumps in the basement to get the water out.

- **Building in the 43rd floor of a high rise building along the San Andreas fault line.** This is not a big deal until a magnitude 7 quake hits the area and you end up with several racks embedded in the walls because the building moves a good five feet in all directions at the level of the 43rd floor. If another space is not available, seismic restraints should be used.

- **Building in a space with the restrooms built right in the middle.** This really happened. The space was shaped like a square donut with the rest rooms occupying a block in the middle. How do you efficiently cool a donut-shaped space? Having toilets in the middle of your data center is not the right way to add humidity to your HVAC system. If you must live with this type of room shape, you must. But if you have any say in the matter, look into other locations.

- **Aisles aren't wide enough for newer or bigger machines.** The people who move the equipment end up ripping massive holes in the walls trying to make the tight turns required to get from the loading dock to the staging area. Maybe a few dozen light fixtures along the corridor are taken out as well. Your building maintenance crews will get very angry when this is done on a weekly basis. Know how much space is needed to move and turn the racks and design in adequate aisle space. This means anticipating larger and heavier machines.

- **Not knowing the structural load rating of raised floors and ramps.** Imagine this: You acquire a space with an existing raised floor and ramps. This means a big chunk of the cost and design process has been taken care of! The day arrives when the storage and server racks begin moving in. Unfortunately, no one checked into the load rating for the floor and ramps. While rolling in a heavy rack, a portion of the floor gives way, taking the rack and several people with it into a big hole. You learn quickly about liability issues. Know the total weight that will go on the floor and ramps, and make sure existing floors and ramps meet these specifications.

Raised Floor

A raised floor is an option with very practical benefits. It provides flexibility in electrical and network cabling, and air conditioning.

A raised floor is not the only solution. Power and network poles can be located on the floor and air conditioning can be delivered through ducts in the ceiling. Building a data center without a raised floor can address certain requirements in ISP/CoLo locations. Wire fencing can be installed to create cages that you can rent out. No raised floor allows these cages to go floor to ceiling and prohibits people from crawling beneath the raised floor to gain unauthorized access to cages rented by other businesses. Another problem this eliminates in an ISP/CoLo situation is the loss of cooling to one cage because a cage closer to the HVAC unit has too many open tiles that are decreasing subfloor pressure. However, some ISP/CoLo locations have built facilities with raised floor environments, because the benefits of a raised floor have outweighed the potential problems listed above.

Drawbacks to the no-raised-floor system are the very inefficient cooling that cannot easily be rerouted to other areas, as well as the problems associated with exposed power and network cabling. A raised floor is a more versatile solution.

Raised floors are covered in more detail in Chapter 6, "Implementing a Raised Floor."

Aisles and Other Necessary Open Space

Aisle space should allow for unobstructed passage and for the replacement of racks within a row without colliding with other racks. The optimal space would allow for the turn radius required to roll the racks in and out of the row. Also, rows should not be continuous. Unbroken rows make passage from aisle to aisle, or from the front of a rack to the back, very time consuming. Such clear passage is particularly important in emergency situations. The general rule of thumb for free floor space is between 40 and 50 percent of the square footage.

FIGURE 3-2 gives an example of an appropriate layout.

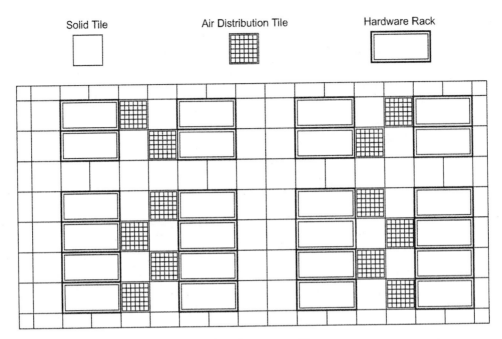

Solid Tile   Air Distribution Tile   Hardware Rack

FIGURE 3-2 Proper Aisle Space and Non-Continuous Rows

How aisle space is designed also depends upon air flow requirements and RLUs.
When designing the center, remember that the rows of equipment should run
parallel to the air handlers with little or no obstructions to the air flow. This allows
for cold air to move to the machines that need it, and the unobstructed return of
heated air back to the air conditioners.

Be sure to consider adequate aisle space in the initial planning stages. In a walls-
within-walls construction where the data center is sectioned off within a building,
aisle space can get tight, particularly around the perimeter.

Command Center

Though an optional consideration, for some companies a separate Command Center
(also called a Command and Control Center) is useful for controlling access to the
consoles of critical systems. This is just one of the many security devices used in the
data center. In disaster recovery scenarios or other critical times, the Command
Center is a key area. In many corporations where computer technology is at the core
of their business, this Command Center also serves as a "war room" in times of
crisis.

However, with companies moving to geographically distributed work forces, having only one way to monitor and work on equipment in the data center might not be a practical alternative. Being able to hire from a talent pool on a global scale increases your chances of getting better people because the pool is larger. This is also useful if you are in an area prone to bad weather. A person might not be able to get into the Command Center, but if the data center is remotely accessible and they have power and a phone line, they can still work.

As more companies move to electronic ways of doing business, Command Centers are becoming public relations focal points. They can be designed as a glassed in box that looks into the computer room to give personnel a way to monitor security and allow visitors a view of the equipment without entering the restricted and environmentally controlled area. If the data center is a key component of the company's image, the Command Center can be designed to look "cool," an important PR tool. Whether it looks into the data center computer room or not, a modern, high tech Command Center room is an impressive location for executives to talk to the press, television, analysts, and shareholders.

From a security standpoint, the Command Center is practical because physical access to the data center can be monitored from within the Command Center and possibly access can be allowed only *through* the Command Center. Since the Command Center could be the only way to connect to the administrative network, logical access to that network can be controlled within the Command Center as well.

Data Center Support Systems

A data center must provide certain services:

- Locations on the floor that can support the weight of the racks
- Power to run the racks
- Cooling to keep the racks from overheating
- Connectivity to make the devices in the racks available to users
- Planned redundancies

If any one of these services fail, the system will not run effectively, or at all. These support systems are how a data center supplies its intended services. They are also interdependent. If you can't place the server in the data center, it won't run. If you can't get enough power to run the server, it won't run. If you can't cool the server, it won't run for long, a few minutes at best. If you can't connect the server to the people who need to use it, what good is it? All of these requirements must be met simultaneously. If one of them fails, they all might as well fail. Your data center can only be as effective as its weakest support system.

Space and Weight

You have to be able to place the servers in the data center and, depending on the type of server, you might need even more space than its physical footprint to cool it. This is the *cooling footprint*. Weight is also a major consideration. If you have space for the machine, but your raised floor can't handle the weight load, it will crash through the raised floor. The ramps or lift you use to get the machine onto the raised floor must also be able to handle the weight load of the system.

Power Requirements

It is essential that the data center be supplied with a reliable and redundant source of power. If computers are subjected to frequent power interruptions and fluctuations, the components will experience a higher failure rate than they would with stable power sources. To assure that power is up constantly, multiple utility feeds, preferably from different substations or power utility grids, should be used. Also, the data center should have dedicated power distribution panels. Isolating the data center power from other power in the building protects the data center and avoids power risks outside your control.

The power distribution system is covered in more detail in Chapter 7, "Power Distribution."

HVAC and Air Flow Requirements

Placement of the HVAC (air conditioning) units is highly dependent on the size and shape of the data center room, as well as the availability of connections to support systems. The primary concern in placement is for optimal effectiveness in dealing with the planned load.

Air flow must be considered in the layout of the HVAC systems as well. Reducing obstructions under the floor will provide the best air flow to the areas where the air is needed. Air flow is also governed by under-floor pressure, so the placement and distribution of solid and perforated tiles on the raised floor should be carefully considered. You must maintain higher air pressure under the floor than in the data center space above the floor.

Air conditioning and HVAC placement is covered in more detail in Chapter 8, "HVAC and Other Environmental Controls."

Network Cabling

Network cabling is essential to a data center. It must supply not only TCP/IP connectivity, but connectivity to Storage Area Networks (SAN) as well. Storage systems are becoming increasingly "network aware" devices. Whether this has to do with managing storage through TCP/IP networks or with using these devices on SANs, the requirements of the network cabling must be flexible and scalable.

Most of these requirements can be met using Cat5 copper and multi-mode fibre. However, some single-mode fibre might also be needed to support WAN requirements. Understanding what equipment will go where and knowing the cabling requirements of each piece of equipment is integral to building data centers. Of all of these support systems, upgrading or adding more network cabling inside the data center is the least intrusive support system upgrade.

Network cabling is covered in more detail in Chapter 9, "Network Cabling Infrastructure."

Planned Redundancies

It is important to consider all of the possible resources that will be needed for redundancy. Particularly, consider redundancy for power and environmental support equipment. Redundant systems allow for uninterrupted operation of the center during electrical and HVAC upgrades or replacements. A new HVAC unit can be run simultaneously with the hardware it is replacing rather than swapping the two. Redundancy assures that power and environmental controls are available in the event of power or equipment failures.

Plan for at least the minimal amount of redundancy, but also plan for future redundancy based on projected growth and changes within the center. Will the focus of the center change from a development to a mission critical facility? Will redundant HVAC units be necessary and, if so, where will they be placed? Should greater capacity electrical wiring be pre-installed for future systems?

It is important that the intentions for redundancy be maintained as the demands of the data center change and grow. Extra floor space or support systems that were planned for redundancy should not necessarily be used for expansion if this strategy means increasing the chances of downtime due to failures. Make sure the blueprints clearly indicate the intended purpose of the space and systems.

The biggest problem with allocating less redundancy to create more capacity is in the area of sub-panel and circuit breaker space. You should allocate space for at least one additional sub-panel and breakers in the mechanical room for each megawatt of power you have in the data center.

Also, consider redundancy for UPS and emergency power generators. While these are large expenditures and twice as large if they are totally redundant, in a mission critical data center where the cost of even one minute of downtime can cost millions of dollars, they could be a prudent investment. Use the resources of your risk analysts to determine the cost-effectiveness of these redundant systems.

Physical and Logical Security

Two types of security must be addressed in the data center design. It is important to limit access of unauthorized people into the data center proper, and to prevent unauthorized access to the network.

Physical Access Restrictions

Access to the data center should be strictly regulated, limited to personnel necessary to keeping the equipment in operation. It should not be necessary for anyone else to enter the data center. Those allowed access should have a clear understanding of the sensitivities of the hardware to avoid accidental contact with buttons, cable connections, terminals, or emergency response controls.

All points of access should be controlled by checkpoints, and coded card readers or cipher locks. Figure 3-3 shows these two restricted access features for entry into secure areas.

FIGURE 3-3 Cipher Lock (Left) and Card Reader (Right) at Restricted Access Doorways

For added security, cameras can be installed at entry points to be monitored by security personnel.

Logical Access Restrictions

The ability to access the physical console of a system over a network has many advantages, including:

- The ability to administer machines in a different region, even a different country
- The ability to work remotely, from house, hotel, or even a conference

However, this also means that anyone on the network could gain unauthorized access to the physical console. Ways to reduce this risk include:

- Creating several levels of authentication
- Placing limits on who can log in to the console servers
- Putting consoles on an administrative network that can be accessed only from the Command Center, and only over authentication through a VPN

Network security is an important issue, but it's not within the bounds of this book to recommend network security practices. There are, however, many articles on the subject at http://www.sun.com/blueprints/online.html. At this website you'll also find information on "The Solaris™ Security Toolkit" by Alex Noodergraaf and Glenn Brunette.

System Monitoring

Monitoring system status, health, and load is a useful tool for understanding how each system is working, by itself and in relationship to other connected systems. It is not within the scope of this book to cover the "how" of system monitoring, as there are many other sources for this information. However, whatever software you use for monitoring should conform to industry standard interfaces like Simple Network Monitoring Protocol (SNMP). Even HVAC systems and UPS systems can be connected to the network and run SNMP agents to give useful information on the health of the data center and support systems.

Remote Systems Management

Remote systems management, like remote access, has many advantages. It offers the ability to work remotely, whether you are snowed in at home or at a hotel attending a conference. It allows you to get the best people available from the largest labor pool. Monitoring and Management systems like Sun™ Management Center (Sun MC), BMC Patrol, and others allow you to monitor and manage devices from pagers and cell phones from anywhere around the world.

Effective systems management is critical to a smoothly running data center, and even more critical when managing remotely. System configuration information (hardware, software, patches, etc.) is the foundation for remote systems management. It is critical that this information be accurate and reliable. Elizabeth Purcell, a Sun performance availability engineering systems engineer, presented a paper on this topic at the October 2001 SuperG conference. For more in-depth information on this subject, see Ms. Purcell's paper reproduced in Appendix A, "Managing System Configurations."

Remote systems management is also handy if you have multiple data centers around the world. For example, you might have data centers in Los Angeles, London, and Tokyo. Each city is 8 hours from the next. The administrative networks at each of these Command Centers have connections to the administrative networks of the other two sites. The London crew has coverage of all systems in all three locations from 9:00 a.m. to 5:00 p.m. GMT. At 5:00 p.m. when the crew in London is done for the day, it is 9:00 a.m. in Los Angeles and the L.A. crew takes the next shift. At 5:00 p.m. in L.A. it is 9:00 a.m. the next day in Tokyo. The Tokyo crew takes over till 5:00 p.m. when the London crew is back at work at 9:00 a.m. London time. This is built-in 24 hour, 7 day a week coverage of all data centers, with no one crew having to work "graveyard" hours.

The biggest disadvantage to remote systems management is the possibility of security violations such as someone cracking into the administrative networks. While tools like firewalls and secure shell can help reduce this risk, it is highly recommended that you have your own data center personnel who specialize in this area of technology. Or, you can outsource this type of work to firms that specialize in data, system, and network security. This flexibility is not without risk and cost; however, you might find that these risk and costs are more than offset by the flexibility and productivity you can achieve through remote systems management.

Planning for Possible Expansion

In general, the next generation of hardware will take up less room for the same and larger computational and storage capacities. Therefore, more capacity can be put into an existing space. However, since computing needs rise faster than computing power, don't expect the space needs of the data center to shrink.

Most data centers have been able to continue within the same area without having to take up more real estate. However, power and cooling requirements increase. Even if you have the physical space to expand, you might not be able to accommodate the additional power or cooling requirements of expansion. Also, sometimes a direct addition to an operational data center is an even a tougher design and construction challenge than building a new facility. What is more likely is that a future expansion would be treated as a separate space from the existing data center, and you can use the networking infrastructure of the existing data center to "link up" the expansion data center with the existing one.

Using RLUs to determine data center capacities is the best method for planning for future expansion. RLUs will give you the tools to define your space, structural needs, in-feeds (including power and cooling), etc. and therefore give you a clear picture of remaining capacities. For more information on defining RLUs, see Chapter 4, "Determining Data Center Capacities."

Determining Data Center Capacities

"Everything is connected to everything else."

- Vladimir Ilyich Lenin

Designing a data center involves many different variables that include the housing structure, all of the utility and network feeds necessary to keep the center operational, and the storage and processing power of the hardware. Balancing all of these variables to design a data center that meets the project scope and keeps the center in constant operation can easily become a hit or miss operation if not carefully planned. Using older methods, such as basing power and cooling needs on square footage, gives inadequate and incomplete results. A newer method looks more closely at room and equipment capacities using rack location units (RLUs) to plan the data center.

This chapter contains the following sections:

- "Data Center Capacities"
- "Purpose of Rack Location Units"
- "Data Center Evolution"
- "Determining Criteria for RLUs"
- "Creating RLU Definitions"
- "Using RLUs to Determine In-Feed Capacities"
- "Planning for Equipment Layout"

Data Center Capacities

The design of the data center is dependent on the balance of two sets of capacities:

- **Data center capacities:** Power, cooling, physical space, weight load, bandwidth (or connectivity), and functional capacities
- **Equipment capacities:** The various devices (typically equipment in racks) that could populate the data center in various numbers

Depending on the chosen site of the data center, one of these sets of capacities will usually determine the other. For example, if the project scope includes a preferred amount of *equipment capacity* for the data center, the knowledge of the equipment requirements can be used to determine the size of the center, the amount of power and cooling needed, the weight load rating of the raised floor, and the cabling needed for connectivity to the network. In other words, the equipment will determine the necessary *data center capacities*. On the other hand, if the data center will be built in a pre-existing space, and this space has limitations for square footage, power, etc., this will determine the supportable *equipment capacities*. In other words, the data center size and in-feeds will determine how much equipment you can put in the data center.

Note – The project scope should include the budget limitations, and these numbers (though not discussed in this chapter) must also be considered.

A new method for designing a data center based on these capacities uses a calculating system called RLUs. The actual process of defining RLUs to determine the capacities of a data center boils down to careful planning. RLUs will assist you in turning the critical design variables of the data center into absolutes. The idea is to make sure the needs of each rack are met as efficiently as possible. RLUs tell you the limits of device requirements and, therefore, the limits of the data center itself. Knowing these limits, no matter how great or small, gives you complete control over the design elements.

Purpose of Rack Location Units

The job of planning the data center is one of balancing. You will add equipment, modify the in-feeds based on the equipment, find the limits to the feeds, reevaluate the equipment population or configuration, find that the budget has changed, then reevaluate equipment and resources.

The Rack Location Unit (RLU) system is a completely flexible and scalable system that can be used to determine the equipment needs for a data center of any size, whether 100 or 100,000,000 square feet. The system can be used whether you are designing a data center that will be built to suit, or using a predefined space. The RLU determinations are a task of the design process and can determine whether or not the space is adequate to fulfill the company requirements. Regardless of limiting factors, RLUs allow you the flexibility to design within them.

Flexibility is the key.

In a data center, most devices are installed in racks. A rack is set up in a specific location on the data center floor, and services such as power, cooling, bandwidth, etc., must be delivered to this location. This location on the floor where services are delivered for each rack is generally called a "rack location." We also use the information on these services as a way to calculate some or all of the total services needed for the data center. Services delivered to any rack location on the floor are a unit of measure, just like kilos, meters, or watts. This is how the term "rack location units" was born.

RLUs are defined by the data center designer based on very specific device requirements. These requirements are the specifications that come from the equipment manufacturers. These requirements are:

- Power (how many outlets/circuits it requires, how many watts it draws)
- Cooling (BTUs per hour that must be cooled)
- Physical space (how much floor space each rack needs, including the cooling dimensions)
- Weight (how much a rack weighs)
- Bandwidth (how it connects to the network)
- Functional capacity (how much computational power, physical memory, disk space, as well as how many spindles, MFLOPS, database transactions, and any other measures of rack functions)

RLUs based on these specifications can be used to determine:

- How much power, cooling, bandwidth, physical space, and floor load support is needed for the racks, alone, in groups, and in combination with other racks
- How many racks and of what configurations the data center and outside utilities can support

Unlike other methods, the RLU system works in both directions: determining necessary resources to accommodate and feed the equipment, and assisting changes in the quantities and configurations of the equipment to accept any limitation of resources.

Data Center Evolution

In the past, there were mainframes. There was usually only one of them for a company or a data center. The mainframe had a set of criteria: How much power it needed, how much heat it would give off per hour, how large it was, and how much it weighed. These criteria were non-negotiable. If you satisfied these criteria, the machine would run. If you didn't, it wouldn't run. You had one machine and you had to build a physical environment it could live in.

Fast forward to the 21st century. Computers have become a lot faster and a lot smaller. The data center that used to house just one machine now holds tens, hundreds, perhaps thousands of machines. But there is something that hasn't changed. Each of these machines still has the same set of criteria: power, cooling, physical space, and weight. There is also an additional criteria: network connectivity. These criteria still need to be satisfied and they are still non-negotiable.

So, now you have different types of servers, storage arrays, and network equipment, typically contained in racks.

How can you determine the criteria for all the different devices from the different vendors? Also, whether you are building a new data center or retrofitting an existing one, there are likely to be some limits on one or more of the criteria. For example, you might only be able to get one hundred fifty 30 Amp circuits of power. Or you might only be able to cool 400,000 BTUs per hour. This is an annoying and frequent problem. Creating RLU definitions will give you numbers to add up to help you decide how many racks you can support with these limitations.

Until recently, data centers were populated with equipment based on using a certain wattage per square foot which yielded an amount of power available to the equipment. This could also be used to roughly determine the HVAC tonnage needed to cool the equipment. Unfortunately, using square footage for these decisions assumes power and cooling loads are equal across the entire room and does not take the other requirements of the racks, or the number of racks, into consideration. This worked when a single machine such as a mainframe was involved. The modern data center generally uses multiple machines and often these are different types of devices with different specifications. There are also different densities of equipment within the different areas of the data center.

For example, consider figure 4-1 which shows a modern data center room layout:

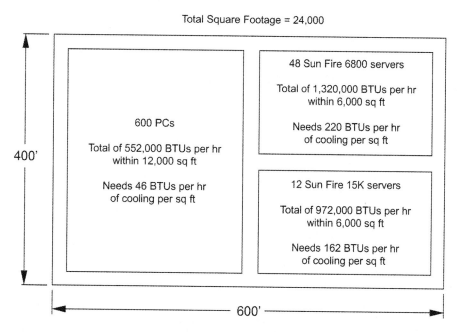

FIGURE 4-1   Using Square Footage to Determine Cooling Needs

The areas represented by dotted lines are areas with different RLU definitions. This is necessary because each of the three sections has its own power, cooling, bandwidth, space, and weight requirements (or limitations).

The previous figure shows only the HVAC requirements as an example. If you total up the cooling needs of all three sections the total is 2,844,000 BTUs per hour. Divide this number by the square footage of the room (24,000 sq ft) and you get 118.50 BTUs per hour of cooling per square foot. This would be far too much for the PCs that need only 46 BTUs per hour of cooling per square foot, but far too little for both the Sun Fire™ 6800 and Sun Fire 15K servers that need 220 and 162 BTUs per hour of cooling per square foot, respectively. Therefore, it's clear that determining the HVAC capacity needed by using the total square footage in the room won't work in most data centers.

This leads us into the new frontier: RLUs.

Determining Criteria for RLUs

Before discussing how RLUs are determined and used, we should examine the six criteria used in the determinations. These are power, cooling, physical space, network connectivity, rack weight, and logical capacity. The following figure shows in-feeds from power, HVAC, and network connectivity. It also shows that the other three criteria, physical space, weight specifications, and functional capacity, are aspects of the rack. Keep in mind that the specifications for these criteria should be listed for the rack or the rack's individual devices. If they are not on hand, you should get them from the equipment manufacturers.

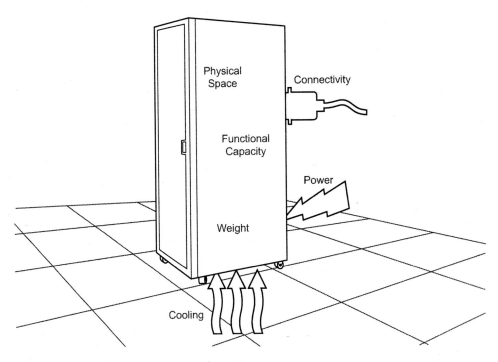

FIGURE 4-2 RLU Criteria

Power

The amount of power, number of breakers, and how the center is wired are all dependent on the needs of the equipment planned to occupy the floor space. When you know the power specifications and requirements of all the devices, you can do the math and begin designing the power system.

You need to know the following:

- What is needed to plug in the rack
- The outlet type
- Its voltage and amperage
- Whether it's single phase or three phase
- How much power the rack will draw

The last item is best described in watts. This information should be part of the manufacturer's specifications. However, if the specifications don't tell you how many watts the device will draw, you can calculate this from the BTUs-per-hour rating of the rack.

BTUs per hour 3.42 = watts

You will also need to know if the rack has redundant power. If so, all watt usage requirements must be multiplied by this value. If the rack has no redundant power, the multiplier is one; if it does have redundant power, the multiplier is two. In an RLU specification, this multiplier is referenced as RM (redundancy multiplier).

Power can be difficult to retrofit, so you should plan carefully for future power needs and install conduit and wiring adequate for future power upgrades.

Cooling

A rack of devices produces heat and requires a specific amount of cooling to keep it running. The HVAC requirements should be carefully planned, because retrofitting the HVAC system is no easy task.

Cooling requirements are specified as BTUs per hour. This should be part of the manufacturer's specifications. If it is not, you can calculate it from the amount of watts the machine uses.

Watts $\times$ 3.42 = BTUs per hour

At minimum, either BTUs per hour or watt usage must be available from the HVAC manufacturer. The requirement is to deliver enough conditioned air to the rack to meet the BTUs per hour requirement. For example, if you have a rack that has a cooling requirement of 10,000 BTUs per hour, and the HVAC system is only able to deliver conditioned air to this rack location at 90 percent efficiency, then it must deliver 11,110 BTUs per hour into the plenum to compensate for this inefficiency. Work with your HVAC contractor to ensure this.

The amount of area (square footage) needed on the floor for each rack must take not only the actual dimensions of the rack into consideration, but also its cooling dimensions. This is the area outside the rack used to draw air to cool the internal components and exhaust this heated air out of the rack and back to the return plenum. While newer Sun racks are usually cooled front-to-back (an efficient use of space because racks can be placed side-by-side), older Sun racks and racks from other manufacturers might draw or expel air at the sides. The dimensions you use in determining RLUs should include this cooling area.

The following figure shows examples of the general cooling dimensions of racks with different air patterns. These dimensions also indicate the minimum areas that should be left unobstructed by other equipment to allow for the free flowing of air. Check with the manufacturer for the actual cooling dimension specifications.

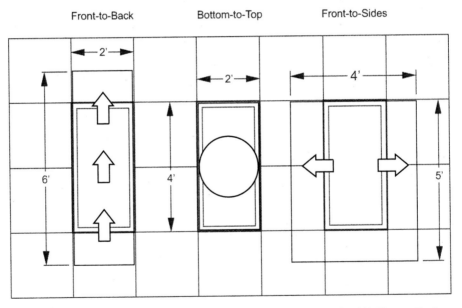

FIGURE 4-3 Possible Cooling Dimensions (Within Dotted Lines) of Different Racks

The cooling space required outside the rack can often be used as aisles and free space. In a front-to-back configuration, the cooling area would be part of the 40 to 50 percent of the total square footage needed for free space.

Bandwidth

The primary concern with bandwidth (connectivity) is the network and storage cabling within the data center. This is usually done with Category 5 (Cat5 - copper) cables and/or multi-mode fibre cables. When determining the bandwidth part of the RLU, the concern will primarily be whether or not there are enough connections for the rack to interface with other devices.

To effectively plan connectivity outside the data center, your ISP service bandwidth should meet or exceed the total capacity of your data center's inbound and outbound bandwidth specifications. The cost of bandwidth goes down over time, so it might not be worth over-provisioning. Putting in the best quality and sufficient quantities of cables for networking and storage up front is recommended, but it might be more cost-effective to buy switches and ports as you need them.

Bandwidth within the data center is the easiest to retrofit. If you must cut costs in the design stages, cut internal cabling first. You can always add it later as budget allows. Cabling to the outside ISP should be done correctly in the beginning because changing this cable is costly (sometimes involving ripping up walls, floors, digging trenches, etc.).

Weight

It is critical that you know not only the individual weights of each type of rack that will reside in the data center, but the combined weight of all of them. With this knowledge, and some forethought as to the future weight that will be added, you can decide whether the existing floor can handle the load. Or, if you are building to suit, you can plan for a subfloor and raised floor that will exceed the weight demands.

Each distinct rack has a specified weight. This weight is generally the same for all racks of the same manufacturer and model, but could change due to additions or subtractions to the configuration. The exact weight, or the potential weight of the rack, should be used in the calculations to ensure a floor that can handle the load. There are a few different floor load capacities to consider:

- **Total floor load.** The weight the entire raised floor structure and subfloor can support. This is particularly important if the subfloor is built on an upper story floor rather than solid ground. Also, the raised floor structure must be chosen with a rating exceeding current and future weight demands.

- **Total tile load.** The weight a single tile of a specific type can support. There are "solid," "perforated," and "grated" tiles. The amount of load that can be handled by these types of tiles can vary widely from one manufacturer to the next, and from one type of tile to the next. Material type and amount of perf are key factors in support strength. Using a typical filled raised floor tile, a 15 percent pass-through tile (meaning that 15 percent of the area of the tile is open space) will be able to handle a higher total load than a 25 percent pass-through tile because less material has been removed. However, cast aluminum tiles can support the same total tile load, sometimes referred to as concentrated load, whether the tile is solid, perforated, or grated. Grated tiles can have up to a 55 percent pass-through.

- **Point load of tile.** The point load of the tile of specific type. A tile should be chosen that will support the worst case point load of all the racks in the room. This is generally a quarter of the weight of the heaviest rack, but the point load should be multiplied by two, and should not exceed the total tile load. It would be rare to have more than two casters from the same rack or a single caster from two racks on a single tile.

Load capacity is probably the most difficult of the criteria to retrofit later. Imagine trying to keep the data center up and running while replacing a raised floor.

Concerns About Weight

The most overlooked area in data centers is floor load ratings. We've now reached a point where high end systems and storage racks are starting to put a strain on existing floor load ratings and the problem is going to get worse. As we get more density in a smaller space, the per tile weight requirements go up drastically. Flooring systems designed for clean room applications are finding their way into data centers, specifically for these reasons. For example, Interface Inc.'s Tri-Tec floor system has a 55 percent pass-through grated cast aluminum tile that can handle a total load of 1,750 PSI.

Budget is often a major factor in determining what type of raised floor you install. In some data center applications, using the same raised floor throughout makes sense. However, there are areas, such as high value storage areas, electrical rooms, or areas with lighter equipment, that might not need such high floor load capacities. For example, the Sun Netra™ X1 server weighs 6kg or 13.2 lbs. A single rack with 30 Netra X1s would weigh less then 500 lbs, and that's assuming the rack itself weighs 100 lbs. A Sun Fire™ 6800 server weighs 1000 lbs. And the Sun Fire 15K server tips the scales at 2200 lbs (yep, that's one metric ton!). Now, if you know that you'll have areas with smaller floor loads, you can use a lower rated floor in that area and save some money on the budget. However, you have designed in a restriction so that equipment in that area cannot exceed a specific weight.

If you decide to split up the weight load of your data center floor, you must also consider the pathway to the higher load area. The heavier rated floor should be the one closer to the entry point. It's poor planning to construct a higher rated floor on the far side of your data center, and a lower rated floor between that floor and the access point, because equipment must be transported over this space.

Physical Space

There are essentially three aspects of physical space to consider when determining the area requirements for a rack:

- The width and depth dimensions of the rack.

- The cooling dimensions of the rack (the physical dimensions plus the extra space needed for intake and exhaust of air as defined by the rack cooling profile). Cooling dimensions are described in the previous "Cooling" section.

- The free space needed for aisles, row breaks, ramps, and free air circulation (typically 40 to 50 percent of the total square footage).

Functional Capacity

Functional capacity is required *only* to determine the quantity and type of RLUs you will need to meet the project scope. For example, a Sun StorEdge™ T3 array might contain 36 gigabyte or 73 gigabyte drives. A fully configured rack of Sun StoreEdge T3 arrays with 36 gigabyte drives has a functional capacity of 2.5 terabyte. A fully configured rack of Sun StoreEdge T3 arrays with 73 gigabyte drives has 5.2 terabyte functional capacity. So, if your project scope specifies 100 terabytes of storage, you would need only 20 Sun StoreEdge T3 arrays with 73 gigabyte drives. Forty would be needed if 36 gigabyte drives are used.

Knowing the functional requirements of the data center falls into the realm of capacity planning which is not usually the role of the data center designer. For in-depth information on capacity planning, the following two Sun BluePrints™ books are recommended: *Capacity Planning for Internet Services* by Adrian Cockcroft and Bill Walker, and *Resource Management* by Richard McDougall, Adrian Cockcroft, Evert Hoogendoorn, Enrique Vargas, and Tom Bialaski. Also recommended is *Sun Performance and Tuning (Second Edition)* by Adrian Cockcroft and Richard Pettit. These books offer excellent information on capacity and performance issues that you should know to do accurate capacity planning. See Appendix B, "Bibliography and References" for more information.

Creating RLU Definitions

An RLU is a way to categorize the set of criteria for a rack of equipment that must be met for it to function. As previously described, these are power, cooling, physical space, weight, bandwidth, and functional capacity.

The RLU tells you exactly what criteria needs to be meet for a rack of equipment to run. It doesn't matter what the empty space (places where machines do not live, aisles, pathways between aisles, door entries, etc.) has as criteria (it could be 90 degrees by the ramp). It also indicates where the physical attributes such as power outlets, cooling air, fibre connection terminations, etc., need to be located. They need to be located wherever the RLU will be located in the data center.

To determine the bandwidth requirements for any RLU, you need to look at how the racks will be connected. The following table shows the RLUs created for three Sun products, Sun StorEdge T3 array for the Enterprise, Sun StorEdge A5200 array, and the Sun Fire 6800 server.

TABLE 4-1   Sample RLUs

Specifications	RLU-A (Sun StorEdge T3 array for the Enterprise)	RLU-B (Sun StorEdge A5200 array)	RLU-C (Sun Fire 6800 server)
Weight	780 lbs (294 kg)	970 lbs (362 kg)	1000 lbs (454.5 kg)
Power	Two 30Amp 208V L6-30R outlets RM = 2 3812 Watts × RM	Two 30Amp 208V L6-30R outlets RM=2 4111 Watts × RM	Four 30Amp 208V L6-30R outlets RM=2 8488 Watts × RM
Cooling	13040 BTUs per hr	14060 BTUs per hr	29030 BTUs per hr
Physical Space	24 in. × 48 in.	24 in. × 48 in.	24 in. × 53 in.
Bandwidth	8 multi-mode fibre	12 multi-mode fibre	4 Cat5 copper 12 multi-mode fibre
Functional Capacity	5.2 TB	4.7 TB	24 CPU 96GB RAM

An individual Sun StorEdge A5200 array has up to four fibre connections. You can fit six Sun StorEdge A5200 arrays in a rack. If your environment only requires you to use two of these four connections (as shown in the table), then 2x6 will give you the correct count. However, if you use all four, the number will be 24. In the case of the Sun Fire 6800 server (RLU-C), the four Cat5 copper connections are necessary for these servers to be connected to two 100BaseT production networks, one administrative network, and one connection to the system processor.

Now you have three RLU definitions: RLU-A, RLU-B, and RLU-C. If you have 30 different racks (all having differing specifications), you would have 30 separate RLUs. This is good, and each type of rack (having different specifications) should have its own RLU designation.

Note – In this example, the definition names are alphabetical, but that only gives 26 possibilities (52 if using both upper and lower case). You can design your own alphanumeric designations. Whatever you choose, keep the designations short.

Notice that the definitions for RLU-A and RLU-B are similar. Power outlets are the same and watt usage is near identical. Cooling is a difference of only 1020 BTUs per hour. Physical space is the same. Weight difference is less then 100 kg. The biggest differences are bandwidth (and that is four fibre connections), and functional capacity at 0.5 terabyte. Therefore, by taking the worst case for each of the criteria you can create a *superset* RLU definition that will meet the requirements of RLU-A and RLU-B. (Keep in mind that a superset definition can combine as many racks as is practical.) For now, let us call this example RLU Superset-A.

TABLE 4-2   Combining Two RLUs Into a Superset RLU

Specifications	RLU Superset-A (Sun StorEdge T3 Array for the Enterprise & Sun StorEdge A5200 Array)
Weight	970 lbs (362 kg)
Power	Two 30Amp 208V L6-30R outlets RM = 2 4111 Watts × 2
Cooling	14060 BTUs per hr
Physical Space	24 in. × 48 in.
Bandwidth	12 multi-mode fibre
Functional Capacity	4.7 TB

Note – Using the "superset" name indicates that an RLU type is made up of the specifications of two or more racks. It is also a good idea to keep a list of the separate RLUs in each superset.

Assume a decision is made to install 60 RLU-A racks and 20 RLU-B racks in your data center. By building 80 RLU Superset-A locations in the data center you can support the 60/20 mix or any mix of 80 RLU-A and RLU-B racks in the data center. That gives you flexibility and leeway if you need to make adjustments.

You now know exactly what you need (power, cooling, etc.) and where you need it for each rack going into the center. Using superset RLUs gives you flexibility in the design if you need to modify the number of racks later, with no need to retrofit.

There is another benefit: Often most data centers are not at full capacity when they are built. By having pre-defined and pre-built RLU locations of given types, you can more easily track the RLU locations that are not in use. As you need to bring new racks online you know exactly how many you can install and where.

Using RLUs to Determine In-Feed Capacities

In-feed capacities are the grand totals of the power, cooling, physical space, weight, and bandwidth you will need to support a given number of racks. Let's say you plan to build a data center with 40 Sun Fire 6800 servers (RLU-C). Each Sun Fire 6800 server will have four Sun StorEdge racks (RLU Superset-A) connected to it. That's 40 RLU-Cs and 160 RLU Superset-As.

The following table shows the total floor load support and in-feed requirements for these RLUs.

TABLE 4-3   Total In-Feeds for Racks

Specifications	40 RLU-C Racks	160 RLU Superset-A Racks	Totals
Weight	40,000 lbs (18,144 kg)	155,200 lbs (70,398 kg)	195,200 lbs (88,542 kg)
Power	160 30Amp 208V L6-30R outlets RM=2 339,506 W × RM = 679,012 W	320 30Amp 208V L6-30R outlets RM=2 657,778 W × RM = 1,315,556 W	480 30Amp 208V L6-30R outlets 1,994,568 W
Cooling	1,161,110	2,249,600	3,410,710
Physical space	24 in. × 53 in. = 360	24 in. × 48 in. = 1280	1,640 sq ft
Bandwidth Cat5: Fibre:	160 320	0 1,280	160 1,600

Only 40 to 60 percent of the floor space in a data center should be used to house machines, as the rest of the space is needed for aisles, row breaks, ramps, etc. Open space is also needed to allow cold air from the floor plenum to come up through perforated tiles to the racks, and for exhaust air to move freely out of the rack and into the HVAC return plenum.

So, multiply the total square footage by 2.0 to get the total square footage needed for the room.

Total Physical Space	=	1,640 sq ft
Usage Multiplier	×	2.0
Total Room Space	=	4100 sq ft

Now we can size our data center, right?

But wait, back the truck up! The architect just informed the electrical engineer that the VP of Human Resources has demanded a larger office and this will only allow us enough circuit breaker panel space for a 450 30A 208V circuit. Now what? We know we need 480 to support all of this equipment. We begged, pleaded, and explained to this VP that we need that space for the panels. No luck. Now it's a matter of reducing the equipment count until the total number of power outlets is reduced from 480 to 450.

Previously, we said that each Sun Fire 6800 server (RLU-C) would have four Sun StorEdge racks (RLU Superset-A) connected to it. The ratio for RLU-C to RLU Superset-A is 4 to 1. So if we remove three RLU-Cs, we remove 3 × 4 thirty Amp 208V or twelve 30Amp 208V outlets. Then we remove twelve RLU Superset-As, 12 × 2 thirty Amp 208V or twenty four 30Amp 208V outlets. This is a reduction of thirty six 30Amp 208V outlets. Now our new breaker panel requirements total 444 30Amp 208V outlets. We can get enough breaker panel space to run these devices.

Remember that the cooling, space, weight, and bandwidth requirements are reduced as well.

Not only do RLUs enable you to know what *services* (power, cooling, etc.) you need and where, they allow you to calculate how much you need. They also allow you to *reverse engineer* the number of racks you can support from any given in-feed limit you might have.

Planning for Equipment Layout

The following describes a possible procedure for planning the equipment set-up and utility feeds for the data center.

1. **Determine what equipment will populate the data center.**

   Based on the project scope (including budget), and working with your capacity planning information, determine what equipment will be connected into the data center. Using your RLUs and capacity planning information, you now have a basis for determining the number of racks needed, as well as their space and utility requirements.

2. **Define RLUs for these racks.**

   Use the information in the previous sections of this chapter to determine RLUs.

3. **Determine maximum utility feeds based on RLUs.**

   Knowing how many RLUs you must accommodate, figure out the following requirements and specifications:

   - Power (number of outlets/type/watts/amps)
   - Cooling (number of tons of HVAC)
   - Space (square footage needed - see the "Cooling" section)
   - Bandwidth (number of copper, number of fibre connections)
   - Weight of racks

4. **Determine the number of RLUs needed to meet the project scope.**

   For example, 25 RLU-X racks require a total of 1.2 megawatts of power and only 900 kilowatts are available. To solve this problem, the designer must make some decisions. Some options are:

   - Get more power (add another 300 kilowatt feed).

   - Get larger drives installed in the racks. The racks will use the same amount of power, but there will be fewer racks needed, thereby decreasing the amount of power needed. This involves changing the RLU definition to change the power-to-capacity ratio.

   - If neither option is available, you have hit a limiting factor.

5. **Determine limiting factors.**

   Possible limiting factors are insufficient power, bandwidth, space, vertical height, and budget.

   - Can the problem be corrected? If so, how much will it cost?
   - Can the scope of the project be modified to accommodate the limitation?
   - If the scope cannot be changed and the limiting factors are not corrected, should the project be abandoned?

6. Begin rough planning of space.

This can be done in many different ways, depending on personal preference. You'll want to visualize where and how many racks you can fit in the space. One way to do this is to get a large plan view of the data center space, usually from a blueprint. Then cut out pieces of paper about the size of your racks and start placing them.

You can also draw directly on the blueprint with colored pens and draw in boxes that represent the racks you need to place, but you'll need several blank copies of the blueprint as you make changes to it. Using a plastic overlay with a grease pencil will make it easier to make corrections.

The most flexible way to plan out the space is with CAD software. Even better, there is facility and technology management software from companies like Aperture (http://www.aperture.com) that allow you to do this type of layout. The advantage of using this type of software is that you can continue to manage the state of the data center using this type of tool, after the data center is built and online. Also Flomerics (http://www.flometrics.com) has software called Flovent that will allow you to do thermal simulations of your data center to see if the layout you are working on will actually cool the racks effectively. See Appendix B, "Bibliography and References" for more information.

CHAPTER 5

Site Selection

"It is my belief, Watson, founded upon my experience, that the lowest and vilest alleys in London do not present a more dreadful record of sin than does the smiling and beautiful countryside."

- Sherlock Holmes, by Sir Arthur Conan Doyle

When housing a data center in an existing building, several design issues must be considered to choose the best location. Careful planning is essential to assure that a location will meet not only immediate needs, but future needs as well. In the event that a building or area must be built to house the data center, there are even more considerations. The build-to-suit option typically offers more flexibility than utilizing an existing area, but careful planning is still essential. Looking ahead and planning the site and layout with forethought can save tremendous amounts of time, money, and aggravation. Poor planning often means costly upgrading, retrofitting, or relocating.

This chapter contains the following sections:

- "Geographic Location"
- "Data Center Site Selection"
- "General Site Considerations"

Geographic Location

Choosing a geographic location for the data center could mean many things. Will the data center be housed in an add-on structure to an existing building? Will a separate building be built? Must property in a remote location be purchased and a new building be built? Will the center be located in a pre-existing building?

Aside from budget, there are several factors, many of which are described below, that should be considered when determining the location of a building site. Consider all of the possible problems with the area. Then, decide which of the problems are necessary evils that must be tolerated, which can be remedied, and which will involve building or retrofitting in such a way as to factor them out.

Potential problems in the geographic location might not be obvious. Resource availability and potential problems, whether natural or man-made, are critical issues and uncovering them requires careful research.

Natural Hazards

The most obvious of potential natural hazards are flooding, tornados, hurricanes, and seismic disruptions such as earthquakes and volcanic activity. If you must locate the data center in an area with a history of these phenomena, make sure you retrofit or build with these hazards in mind. Obviously, a determination must be made whether or not it is financially worthwhile to locate the center in an area with potential hazards. If the site can be set up in such a way that nullifies the problem (for example, in the case of earthquakes, using seismic restraints on the equipment), then it might be worthwhile.

Flooding

Consider whether or not the site is at the bottom of a hill that would catch rain or snow melt. Is the site on a flood plain? Is it near a river that might overflow? Is the site in the basement area of an existing location? While you are at it, you might as well consider tsunamis.

Seismic Activity

Anything that shakes the building is bad for equipment. Is the potential site in an area that has frequent earthquakes, volcanic activity, or gigantic prehistoric lizards stomping about? What is the seismic history of the area? How often and how severe is the activity? What precautions can be used against the vibration and possible structural damage that can be caused by tremors?

Tornados and Hurricanes

As with seismic activity, what is the history of these phenomenon in the area? What measures can be taken to prevent them from causing damage to the facilities? Is it worth the risk?

High Winds

This might be a concern if you are locating the data center in any of the higher floors of a tall building. If you intend to put the center on the 57th floor of a building in downtown Chicago, you might reconsider unless the building is built to resist moving in high winds.

Temperature Extremes

It is important that data center equipment stay within a specific operational temperature range. In areas with extreme levels of heat or cold, it might be necessary to have more HVAC and insulation. In these areas, humidification is also a problem, and larger humidification units might be necessary. Larger HVAC systems might be worth the cost.

Fire

Though arson is a concern, fires can also occur naturally or accidentally. Consider the history of local fire hazards. Is the site near a wooded or grassy area? Are there lightning storms? Is the building fireproof or fire resistant? Can the building be designed or retrofitted to be fireproof? Can the center be located well away from any facilities where chemicals might create a combustion problem?

Man-Made Hazards

Nature isn't the only culprit in compromising the integrity of data centers. There are also many hazards created by man to disrupt your hard work. Some of them are described in the following sections.

Industrial Pollution

If possible, avoid locating the facility near major sources of industrial pollution. Look carefully at neighboring facilities such as:

- Factories
- Manufacturing facilities
- Sewage treatment plants
- Farms

If chemicals associated with these facilities migrate into the controlled areas of the data center, they can seriously impact not only the hardware, but the health of personnel. The chemicals used in the field treatment of agricultural areas can also pose a threat to people and machines. Though a natural problem, also consider sand and dust that might be blown into the center.

If you must locate in an area with these potential problems, consider this in your design plans for the center. Make sure you use a filtration system robust enough to filter out any local contaminants.

Electromagnetic Interference

Be aware of any surrounding facilities that might be sources of electromagnetic interference (EMI) or radio frequency interference (RFI). Telecommunications signal facilities, airports, electrical railways, and other similar facilities often emit high levels of EMI or RFI that might interfere with your computer hardware and networks.

If you must locate in an area with sources of EMI or RFI, you might need to factor shielding of the center into your plans.

Vibration

Aside from natural vibration problems caused by the planet, there are man-made rumblings to consider. Airports, railways, highways, tunnels, mining operations, quarries, and certain types of industrial plants can generate constant or intermittent vibrations that could disrupt data center operations. Inside the center, such vibrations could cause disruption to data center hardware, and outside the center, they could cause disruption of utilities.

If constant vibration is a problem in the area, you should weigh the possibility of equipment damage over the long term. In the case of occasional tremors, you might consider seismic stabilizers or bracing kits which primarily keep the racks from tipping over.

Emergency Services and Vehicle Access

Are fire and police services in close proximity to the site? What is their response time to the site? Emergency services also include support services such as emergency power generation, air conditioning vehicles, and network service providers.

It is important, particularly in congested urban areas, that there be unobstructed access and parking for emergency vehicles. All possibilities should be examined in the planning stages because emergency situations can and will happen. The personnel of one major company in Chicago was kept out of the building for two days due to a chemical spill from an overturned truck. At another major company, the main access road was blocked by fallen trees. There was no chain saw readily available, so no one could get into the center for a long time. Such situations should be considered in disaster planning, but comprehensive lights-out management can help mitigate such problems. So can having a chainsaw.

Beyond emergency situations, there should also be easy access to loading areas for large delivery vehicles. There should be plenty of room for the trucks to get in and out, pass one another, and to turn around.

Utilities

Make sure the district provides adequate power, water, gas, and any other necessary utilities. Are there redundant feeds from the electrical supplier? Is there an adequate Internet infrastructure in the area? Extreme rural areas might be more problematic in supplying the necessary utilities or assuring consistent uptime.

Data Center Site Selection

Whether the data center will be a dedicated facility or part of a multipurpose building, the physical location is very important. Knowing the scope of the center is essential in making this decision, because many factors come into play. Flexibility is also key to the decision. All of the data center systems must be coordinated with the building systems for the overall support of operations.

The location of the center must be based on numerous criteria, including those discussed in the following sections.

FIGURE 5-1 Data Center Before the Walls, Raised Floor, and Equipment Are Installed

Retrofitting an Existing Site

Building to suit is not always an option. Locating the data center in an existing site could be very different than building a data center site to suit your needs. With an existing area, you must decide whether or not it meets the requirements of the company. Certain factors might make the area unacceptable, such as clumsy size, difficult access for large equipment or vehicles, the inability to control access, or overhead water pipes.

If you are faced with making a choice between locations or determining the viability of a site, you should consider the following questions:

- What is the general layout of the area?
- Is there enough room for required equipment?
- What is the proximity of the area to chillers and condenser units?
- Is there adequate access for moving in and rotating large equipment?
- Where will HVAC units be placed? Inside the area? Outside?
- What are the possibilities for controlling access?
- Is the area isolated from contaminants and liquid leaks?
- Is there room for future expansion?
- Can walls be removed without creating structural instability?
- Can walls be added?
- Can a raised floor be added?
- Is the floor-to-ceiling height adequate for a raised floor, ceiling plenum, and equipment height?
- Will the existing subfloor be able to handle the weight load?
- Is there space for a separate Command Center?

Security

Not all businesses have a need for high-level security, but most businesses must make sure their data centers are secure from vandalism, industrial espionage, and sabotage. Make sure the potential area is situated so that access can be controlled. In a pre-existing building, check for problem areas like ventilators, windows, and doorways that lead directly outside or into an uncontrolled area. Could these openings be a breach to security? Can they be blocked or can access be controlled in another way? Can motion detectors and alarm systems be placed to increase security?

Some siting considerations might include:

- A separate control room and remote access to the systems to minimize the traffic through the data center.
- Locate the data center inside the existing building so there are no exterior windows or doors.
- Avoid sites with windows leading to uncontrolled areas.
- Design the area to limit and control access.
- Make sure the design includes surveillance cameras, motion detectors, and alarms.
- In situations where you must share data center space with other companies, an effective means of segregating the space should be considered.
- Make sure the design includes fast-acting fire control such as FM200.

Also consider the possibility of vandalism by disgruntled employees and accidents that could be caused by the actions of untrained personnel.

Access

Aside from security access considerations, the potential site for the data center should be set up for the loading and unloading of large items such as HVAC units and computer racks. In the case where the data center is not in direct proximity to a loading dock, there must be a way to get bulky equipment to the site. It might also be necessary for small vehicles like forklifts and pallet jacks to have access.

Access considerations might include:

- Area for a loading dock
- Freight elevators
- Wide doorways
- Wide aisles
- Wide hallways
- Ramps at floor-level height changes
- Adequate turning radius space for racks and vehicles
- Adequate space at corner and column areas
- RLU design to ensure open pathways within the data center

Problem areas might include:

- Stairways
- Tight corners
- Low ceilings and overhangs
- Floors with poor load capacities
- Numerous changes in floor height
- Oddly shaped spaces
- No way to make the existing area secure

Raised Flooring

If the data center will have a raised floor, look at the space with some idea of what will be placed beneath it. Consider the following:

- How high can the floor be raised?
- Consider the amount of open plenum necessary to channel air for cooling. Too little space will cool inadequately, too much space will cool inefficiently.
- Are there structural items in place that might obstruct the free flow of air below the floor?
- How will wiring, cabling, and outlets be run?

- Is a raised floor a viable option for the available space?
- With the reduced space between floor and ceiling, is there enough space to get heated air from equipment back to the returns of the HVAC units?

Isolation From Contaminants

Isolate the data center from contaminants or contaminant-producing activities. Avoid locating the center near print rooms, machine shops, wood shops, loading docks, and areas that involve the use of chemicals or generate toxic vapors or dust. Make sure the exhaust from generators or other sources of exhaust do not enter the intakes of air handlers serving the data center. If the data center must be located near these hazardous locations, adequate filtering systems must be added to the design. Also, maintenance schedules for the filtering system should be more frequent.

Risk of Leaks

Liquids pose another serious hazard to data center equipment. Despite precautions, water pipes and water mains can leak or burst. If you plan to locate the data center at a pre-existing site, make sure you know where all water pipes, valves, pumps, and containments are located. If pipes with flowing liquids are running through the ceiling, you might want to consider a different site. Also, will the data center be under floors occupied by other tenants who might have facilities with the potential of creating leaks?

If you must locate the center where there is a risk of leaks, make sure you design in a way to move water out of the room. Consider troughs under the pipes that are adequate to handle the water from a pipe failure and will carry the water out of the room without overflowing. Also make sure there is an emergency water shut-off valve readily accessible in the event of a pipe failure.

Environmental Controls

The type of air conditioning system chosen for the data center, and the location of the units, might determine the viability of a location. Chilled water units must be connected to chillers located in the building or an adjoining support facility, and might require cooling towers. Due to noise and structural issues, chillers are usually located in a basement, separate wing of the building, on the roof, in a parking lot, or in a separate fenced-in area. Direct expansion air conditioners require condenser units located outside the building. Also, the roof or outside pads should be structurally adequate to support the condensers.

Room for Expansion

Anticipating future expansion needs can be a challenge since it is difficult to predict future trends in equipment. As technology advances, it tends to make hardware more space-efficient (though more power and cooling consumptive). Over time, you might fit more equipment into less space, avoiding the need for more floor space (though it might necessitate more power and HVAC capacity which would need floor space). Also, networking allows for expansion in a different place inside the building or in a nearby building. Another separate data center can be built, can be connected logically to the other networks, and therefore to machines in the original data center.

If the need for more space is anticipated, consider this in your plans. Try not to land-lock the center. If building an addition to the existing structure will eventually be necessary, consider how the new area might share the existing support equipment, like chilled water loops, security, etc. If expansion is likely and budget allows, consider putting in the addition with raised floors and using the space for temporary offices or storage.

General Site Considerations

As with any aspect of data center design, the number of questions you can ask yourself about site selection can be almost endless. As food for thought, the following sections list a few questions and ideas you might consider for both geographic (district) and specific (room) locations.

Geographic and District Criteria

Where in the world will the data center be located? Many geographic factors must be considered in the placement and design of the data center. Will the system be installed on the 56th floor of a high-rise in earthquake country? Are there enough skilled people in the local hiring pool? Is there adequate power, or will it be necessary to build a power generator? Consider the following:

- What is the local hiring pool like?
  - Does the district offer adequate technical employee resources?
  - Is the area conducive to employee relocation? Will employees want to live there for a while?

- What is the local power situation?
  - Is there adequate power? Are there redundant grids?
  - Historically, how often does the power fail? For how long?
- Is there adequate connectivity to the Internet or intranet? Does such an infrastructure exist?
  - How many lines of the type needed (for example, T1 or DS3) are available? How soon will they be available?
  - What types of local services are available? Is there access to adequate bandwidth?
- Is there a history of natural disasters in the area?
  - Are there earthquakes?
  - Are there tornados or hurricanes?
  - Is there runoff from rain and/or snow melt?
  - Will flooding be a problem?
  - Are there lightning storms?
  - How cold does it get? How hot?

Data Center Area Criteria

The area is the specific location, the room or rooms, possibly even multiple floors, that will become the data center. Consider the following:

- Is the data center area protected from weather and seismic problems?
- Is the area safe from flooding (not near a river that overflows, in a flood plain, at the bottom of a hill)?
- How will the data center be used?
  - Will it be used for production, testing, information access?
  - Will equipment or racks be rotated?
  - How available must the equipment be (how often online)?
- What security level must there be for data center access?
- Will there be a separate Command Center? Will it be in a separate location than the data center? Where?
- What area is available? What is its shape (round, rectangular, square, L-shaped, T-shaped)?
- How will the area be divided? Consider walls, storage, a Command Center, offices, other rooms, loading docks, etc.
- If built within a multi-level building, what floor or floors will be included and what parts of them are available?

- Is there enough width in the corridors, aisles, doorways, etc. to move large equipment and vehicles?
- Are floors, ramps, etc. strong enough to support heavy equipment and vehicles?
- Is there a nearby loading dock? Is it on the same floor?
- Is a separate site needed for loading, unloading, and storage?
- How much room is left for data center equipment?
- Are there freight elevators? How many?
- Are there passenger elevators? How many?
- Is the area safe from seismic activity (earthquakes, hurricanes, high winds)?
- Are there any water system (bathrooms, kitchens) or pipes above the area?
- Are there necessary facilities such as restrooms and break rooms available?
- Is food available, even if from a vending machine? This is important for people working late or in emergency situations where leaving the area for long periods of time is not possible. Consider a small kitchen in a Command Center.

CHAPTER 6

Implementing a Raised Floor

"Consent upon a sure foundation."

- Lord Bardolph in Henry IV, Part II by William Shakespeare

The purpose of a raised floor is to channel cold air from the HVAC units and direct it up where it's needed to cool equipment, act as an out-of-the-way area to route network and power cables, and act as a framework for equipment grounding. It also provides a *sure* foundation for data center equipment.

This chapter contains the following sections:

- "Anatomy of a Raised Floor"
- "Floor Load Capacity"
- "Air Flow and Pressure"
- "Fire Rating"
- "Local Building Code"

Anatomy of a Raised Floor

A raised floor is generally constructed on a grounded framework, with a load surface of two-foot square tiles (also called panels). The space beneath the floor is called the *plenum*. Feeding conditioned air directly from the HVAC units into the plenum is simple, and gives the flexibility to channel air, in varying degrees, to the locations where it is needed. The plenum is also generally used to route cables and mount electrical outlets that feed right up to the racks. This plan keeps the cabling out of the way, eliminating the possibility of people tripping over them, or accidently unplugging a vital system.

Floor Height

The height of the floor depends on the purpose of the room. Height should be based on air conditioner design and anticipated subfloor congestion. A typical floor height between the subfloor and the top of the floor tiles is 24 inches (61 cm), though a minimum height could be 18 inches (46 cm). The floor height could go as high as 60 inches (152 cm) but, of course, you would need added HVAC to pressurize such a large plenum. The height of the floor is also relative to the total height of the floor space. A 14-foot vertical space with a 5-foot high raised floor leaves only nine feet. This doesn't allow enough ceiling height for air return.

Support Grid

The support grid for the floor has several purposes. It creates the open structure below the floor to allow for the routing of cables, supports the load surface (tiles) and equipment, and is used for part of the "signal reference grid." There are many types of support grids from different manufacturers.

The following figure shows a recommended system that utilizes bolted stringers and provides maximum rigidity for dynamic loads.

FIGURE 6-1 A Floor Grid System With Pedestals, Stringers, and Tiles

If you intend to use an alternative system, such as snap-on stringers, make sure you research them carefully to ensure that they meet the necessary load and stability specifications.

If the data center is to be located in a seismically active area, seismic bracing should be considered for the raised floor system. Verify that the floor manufacturer supplies supplemental bracing before making the decision to use a particular system. If this is not an option, bracing systems are available from several manufacturers that could work with existing equipment.

When determining the type and specifications of the support grid you must anticipate all the possible weight that could be placed on it at one time. Racks full of equipment, HVAC units, equipment on dollies, forklifts or floor jacks, a tour of people, etc. The weight specifications of the floor must exceed this potential weight.

Floor Tiles

A raised floor is typically constructed on a grounded framework, with a load surface consisting of interchangeable tiles (sometimes called floor panels). The tiles can be solid, perforated, or grated. There are many different types of floor tiles, designed for different loads, and to either prohibit air flow or allow specific amounts of air flow through them. Some tiles have custom cutouts for cable or utility passage. There is a great deal of flexibility for designing air flow patterns using tiles with specific air flow characteristics. Solid tiles can be placed to redirect air flow and create subfloor pressure. Perforated tiles can be placed to redirect air flow while also letting a certain percentage of the air flow up into the room or directly into equipment racks.

Tile Construction

Floor tiles are typically 24 in. × 24 in. (61 cm × 61 cm). Historically, the tile cores have been made of compressed wood, concrete, or an open structural metal design. These tiles usually have a point load of 500 pounds. While there are solid tiles from certain manufacturers that allow a load higher than 500 pounds, you should make sure your stretcher system is also rated to handle this type of load. Even if these solid tiles and stretchers can support higher floor load ratings, perforated tiles might not. The use of perforated tiles that can handle higher loads might be required for heavy, bottom-cooled equipment.

Choose tiles based on structural integrity and specific load requirements. Wood or concrete might not support heavier loads. Sun Microsystems Enterprise Technology Centers are now installing cast aluminum tiles to handle the floor loads. These tiles can support a point load of over 1,500 pounds, whether the tiles are solid, perforated, or even grated tiles with a 55 percent pass-through.

The following figure shows an example of a cast aluminum tile.

FIGURE 6-2 Perforated Cast Aluminum Floor Tile Set Into the Support Grid

---

Note – It is best to use tiles with adequate load specifications so they don't warp or become damaged. If this happens, replace them immediately. An ill-fitting tile can pose a safety hazard to people and equipment.

The floor surface must allow for the proper dissipation of electrostatic charges. The floor tiles and grid systems should provide a safe path to ground through the tile surface, to the floor substructure and the signal reference grid. The top surface of the floor covering to understructure resistance should be between a minimum of 1.5 x 105 ohms and a maximum of 2 x 1010 ohms (as per NFPA 56A Test Method). The tile structure (not the surface laminate) to understructure resistance should be less than 10 ohms.

Never use carpeted tiles. Carpets can harbor contaminants that are agitated every time someone walks on the tiles. These tiles are more easily damaged by the movement of hardware, or when removed using specially designed tile lifters that incorporate spikes to catch the loops of the tiles. Also, carpeted tiles designed with static dissipative properties can become less effective over time.

Tile Customizations

Some tiles must be modified to fit around columns, accommodate odd room shapes, or to allow access for conduits, pipes, and cables. All modifications to tiles should be done according to the manufacturer's recommendations and guidelines. The exposed cut edges of all cut-outs must be capped with custom corners or protective trim for the safety of people handling the tiles, to avoid damage to cables, and to optimize the air pressure under the floor. Exposed corners can also shed particulate matter into the airstream.

Additional structural support might be necessary, especially where partial tiles are installed along walls, around columns, or by air conditioners.

For information on floor tile maintenance, see the manufacturer's specifications.

Plenum

A plenum (pronounced PLEH-nuhm, from Latin meaning "full") is a separate space provided for air circulation, and primarily to route conditioned air to where it is needed in the data center. It is typically provided in the space between the subfloor and raised floor, and between the structural ceiling and a drop-down ceiling. The plenum space is often used to house data and power cables. Because some cables can introduce a toxic hazard in the event of fire, special plenum-rated cables might be required in plenum areas. This is subject to local fire code.

Wireways and Outlets

An efficient method of bringing power to the racks on the floor is to put the power under the floor where it is needed. Beneath the floor tiles are outlets set into a wireway which is usually a long metal box that houses the electrical wiring and outlets. The power cables from the racks drop down through cutouts in the tiles and plug into these outlets. The outlets are connected back to circuit breakers and sub-panels by electrical wiring. You could run power cables from each breaker in a sub-panel out to the floor, but the problems of messy cabling under the floor, air flow blockages, and vertices would develop. Centralizing the runs of this electrical wiring to a few areas helps reduce this problem.

Also, power outlets need to be attached to something. A wireway is a combination of conduit housing and a place to secure outlets. Once you know where machines will be on the floor, you know where to place the wireway. Also, using your RLU definitions for each location, you know exactly how many outlets, and of what type, should go to those specific locations on the floor. Your electrical engineer and electrical contractors can then size the wireways accordingly. You want the wireways to be as small as possible, for the least amount of air flow blockage, but they must meet local electrical codes.

The following figure shows an example of a raised floor system. It shows the tile surfaces, plenum (open air space), pedestals, cable tray, and the outlets set into a wireway. It also shows the concrete subfloor.

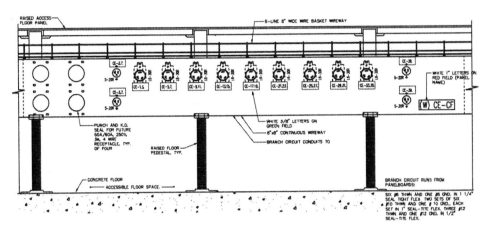

FIGURE 6-3   Blueprint Plan of a Raised Floor

Cable Trays

To keep cables out of harm's way, it is normal to run cables under the raised floor. While many data centers just drop the cables down into the floor, this causes quite a lot of cabling chaos (not so affectionately known as "spaghetti") under the floor. This tangle makes tracing bad cables difficult and time-consuming. Also, large numbers of cables will create air flow obstructions in the raised floor. These obstructions inhibit the free flow of air in the under-floor plenum and decrease under-floor pressure past these blockages. See Chapter 9, "Network Cabling Infrastructure" for more details.

The use of cable trays under the floor serves as a way to organize cables and limit blockages under the floor. The cable trays are generally U-shaped wire baskets (sometimes called "basket wireways") that run parallel to the wireway that houses the electrical outlets. In many cases, these trays will be joined to this wireway, either on top of the wireway or on the opposite side of the outlets. This minimizes air vertices under the floor that can lead to decreased air pressure.

Note – Make sure you factor in at least one and a half inches of space between the top of the cable tray and the bottom of the raised floor tiles to keep the cables from getting crushed. Two inches or more is preferable, but this space could be dependent on the depth of the plenum.

Placement of Wireways and Cable Trays

Before final design plans are completed, you should determine the layout of racks on the raised floor. This will tell you where the fronts and backs of the machines will be and, therefore, which aisles will be cool (intake) aisles and which will be hot (exhaust) aisles. After you know the position of the racks, you can determine precisely where the electrical wireways for your outlets will be placed and on which side of the wireways the outlets will be. It is often standard procedure for an electrician to orient all of the outlets for all of the cable trays in the same direction, unless directed to do it differently.

The following figure shows examples of a few possible options for wireway orientation.

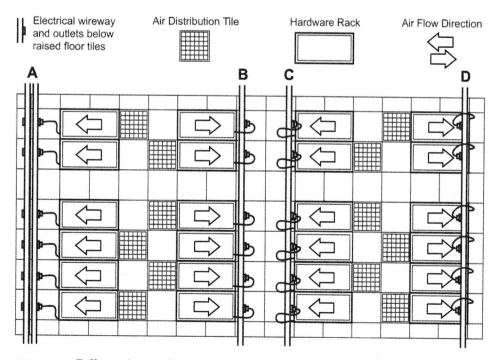

FIGURE 6-4 Different Layout Plans for Wireways

This placement is critical. Poor planning could set things up so that the rack is on top of a tile that covers the outlet and the outlet is facing the wrong direction. Good planning can save you from having to move a machine or crawl under the raised floor to plug in a rack.

This is also a good time to determine where the under-floor cable trays will be installed. The cable trays help organize the network and storage cables and keep them out of the plenum where they would block air flow. Excess power cords should also be placed there.

- **Layout A:** This shows a back-to-back electrical wireway configuration. You could put the cable tray in the middle. You will still have quite a bit of dangling cable because the outlets are far from the server. This will work only if your RLU definitions have very few network and storage cables defined in them.

- **Layout B:** This is probably the most efficient layout. The wireway and outlets are arranged so they can be accessed by removing a tile from the aisle area. The run length from the outlet is shorter than Layout A. Excess cable can be placed in a cable tray, either on the opposite side of the outlet or on the top of the wireway.

- **Layout C:** If you don't look at these types of details in the design process, you could find yourself faced with Layout C for every other row of equipment in your data center. Even though you can lift the tile to get access to the wireway, you will still have to get to the other side to plug it in. If you like working with flashlights and mirrors you could use this layout, but it doesn't fit the "simple" part of the design philosophy.

- **Layout D:** This is the worst of the four layouts. The outlet is not only in the wrong orientation, but it is also under a floor tile that has a rack on top of it. You would have to move the machine two feet to get the tile up to access the outlet. Why is it mentioned here? Because this mistake sometimes happens and now you know to avoid it.

The following are things to consider when planning this layout:

- Does code dictate how the wireways must be placed?

- Will there be adequate space between the top of the cable tray and the bottom of the raised floor tiles? This is important to keep all cabling in the tray from getting crushed. An absolute minimum of 1.5 inches is recommended between the bottom of the raised floor tile and the top of the wireway or cable tray, whichever is higher.

- Can you get to the cabling below the floor without having to move any racks? (Moving racks that are in service is not an option.)

- What is the best layout so that the excess electrical cable can be placed in the wireway without spilling over the sides?

It might be a good idea to create a mock-up using whatever materials work best for you, from coffee stirring sticks and sugar cubes to 2×4s and cardboard boxes, to figure out the best layout for the wireways.

Routing Wires and Cables

There are four different types of cabling in a data center. The first two types are installed during the construction phase. Once these cables are installed, they should not be changed, except by professionals.

- **Power wiring from breakers to outlets.** These go in the wireways under the raised floor.

- **Network "home run" cabling from points of distribution (PODs) on the floor to the network room.** These cables should be bundled together, and their run to the network room should be routed above the raised floor. To maximize air flow under the raised floor, these are usually routed in a separate cable tray in the ceiling plenum.

The second two types of cabling are installed and removed along with racks on the floor by data center personnel. They are routed along the cable trays under the raised floor.

- **Power cables to the racks.** These are the power cables for the racks that come up through a cabling access in the raised floor from the power outlets.

- **Network cables from network PODs to devices.** These cables connect devices to PODs, or connect devices to other devices.

FIGURE 6-5 Neatly Routed Cables (No Spaghetti)

Ramps and Lifts

There are two methods for getting equipment up onto the raised floor: ramps and lifts.

Ramps are the most common. The structural integrity and angle of the ramp are the two biggest factors. Ramps usually go from outside the data center to the staging area. The ramp must not only support the weight of the equipment, but the weight of the pallet, packing materials in which the equipment is shipped, and the weight of the mechanical device used to move the pallet. Mechanical devices are usually hand or electrical powered pallet jacks. Electrical pallet jacks can easily weigh 800 pounds by themselves. Add that to a 2,200 pound Sun Fire 15K server with packing materials, pallet, etc., and the load weighs over 3,000 pounds. That's *one and half tons*. But wait, that's not all! Add a motorized pallet jack and two or three people to maneuver the pallet jack, open doors, etc., and the ramp is now supporting a rolling load of close to 4000 pounds, or *two tons*. It is a good practice to have a fully qualified structural engineer looking into this construction detail.

The scale of the ramp must also be considered. These can range from 1 in 12 (that's 1 inch of rise for every 12 inches of length—a pretty steep ramp) to 1 in 20. A ratio of 1 in 20 is probably more suited to moving large equipment. But, a 1 in 20 ramp for a 24-inch raised floor must be at least 40 feet long. Also, there should be level space at the top and bottom of the ramp to ensure that the pallet jack is in the correct alignment. Add a minimum of 8 feet on each end for that and you have a ramp section 56 feet long. It will probably be 10 feet wide. That's 560 square feet of space just for the ramp.

Building a ramp to support your data center is not a trivial task. Some sites are building ramps with poured concrete. This is not as absurd an idea as it might seem. As previously described, a Sun Fire 15K server with packing material and a motorized pallet jack weighs over 3400 pounds. The unladen weight of a 2002 BMW 330i sedan is 3285 pounds. If your ramp can't handle the weight load of that BMW, it can't handle the weight load of that Sun Fire 15K server.

Lifts are platforms placed on the edge of the raised floor and can raise the equipment to the height of the raised floor surface. While lifts can save space, they are a more expensive alternative. Also, a lift will only be so large, once you size the lift, that is the size of the largest thing you can lift with it. Remember to choose lifts that will accommodate both the size of the pallet jacks you will use and the people operating them. Also, you will be subject to local code restrictions. Code might dictate that you must have a ramp as well as a lift.

Floor Load Capacity

One of the most important issues to be concerned with in the early stages of the data center design is *weight*. It is important to know how much load will be placed on the raised floor so that a support grid and tiles with an adequate load rating can be ordered. Careful planning at this stage is critical. You want to plan for the weight you'll place on the floor today, and the weight you'll place on the floor in the future. Remember: *Once you install the raised floor, it's going to stay there.* Changing out a raised floor in an online data center is a monstrous and costly job. Plan for a raised floor stretcher system and tiles with higher than necessary load ratings.

If you know exactly what equipment you'll be putting on the raised floor and where on the floor you'll be placing the equipment, acquiring tiles and the stretcher system with the correct load capacity is straightforward. Part of the strength of a raised floor is in the fact that each stretcher is connected to four other stretchers in different directions. If you have to replace the tiles and stretcher system of a raised floor, the removal of even a portion of the raised floor would cause weakness in the rest of the floor.

Load capacity won't be much of an issue for ramps made of poured concrete, but it will be for raised floors and structural ramps. There are three types of loads you should consider:

- **Point load.** Most racks sit on four feet or casters. The point load is the weight of a rack on any one of these four points. For example, a Sun Fire 15K server is 2200 pounds with four casters, so the load distribution is 550 pounds per caster. A floor tile must have higher than 550-pound point load, which means that for a 1-inch square area on the tile must be able to support 550 pounds on that 1-inch area without deflection of more than 2 mm.

- **Static load.** Static load is the additive point loads on a tile. If you have two racks, each with a 400 pound point load, and each rack has one caster on a tile, this tile will have a 800 pound static load. The tile must be rated for at least an 800 pound static load.

- **Rolling load.** Rolling load should be close to static load and is usually only applicable to perforated tiles. Since it is possible that you might use your cool aisle to also serve as an aisle to move equipment, the perforated tiles will need to support the weight of two point loads of a rack as they are rolled along the aisle. If the perforated tiles cannot accommodate this load, you would have to temporarily replace them with solid tiles. This would prohibit proper air flow from the cool aisle, and adds work every time you need to move a rack.

The load rating of the raised floor will depend on the design and purpose of the room. Historically, most raised floors were constructed out of concrete-filled steel-shelled floor tiles. While solid tiles might be able to support the current and near future load requirements, the perforated tiles cannot. The strength of these tiles rely on the concrete fill, and perforations in the concrete greatly weaken the tile. Sun's Enterprise Technology Centers have switched to aluminum floor tile systems. These tiles can handle a point load of 1,750 pounds even on a perforated grate with 55 percent air flow. The static load of the same tile is 3,450 pounds.

In a pre-existing building, the structural floor must be assessed to determine whether or not it will support the predetermined weight. Areas designed for light duty, such as offices, might not be able to handle the load. This determination should be made by a qualified structural engineer.

Air Flow and Pressure

Calculating air flow and the amount of air pressure needed to cool the data center involves a number of factors:

- The initial temperature of the air.
- The initial pressure (velocity) of the air.
- How much cooling is needed per rack. (Is it the same for all racks, or do some racks need more cooling than others?)
- The arrangement of solid and perforated tiles (in different perforation percentages) to deliver air at the correct pressure to each rack.

The following figure shows an example of how pressure (in this case, water) diminishes as it is systematically leaked. The example shows a hose with three identically sized holes. The greatest amount of water pressure is leaked from the first hole. The pressure from the second hole is less, and the pressure from the third hole is less still.

FIGURE 6-6   Reduction of Pressure With Distance

In the case of air travelling through a plenum and escaping through the holes of the floor tiles, the same principle applies even if you use only perforated tiles with the same pass-through percentage. The air escaping through the holes of the tile closest to the source (HVAC unit) will move at a greater pressure than the air escaping through the holes in subsequently placed tiles. Therefore, racks directly above the first perforated tile will receive more cooling than racks above perforated tiles farther down the plenum. The last rack in the line might not receive enough air for proper cooling.

To regulate the air more efficiently, perforated tiles of different air flow percentages can be used. The first tiles would have fewer holes relying on the greater pressure to move the required volume into the racks. Subsequent tiles would have more holes to allow volume to move through them despite the drop in pressure.

Solid tiles can also be used to control air flow. Where no air is needed (areas with no racks above them and in the hot aisles in a back-to-back cooling model), solid tiles should be used to maintain the optimum pressure. Or perforated tiles can be placed in locations with no racks if air pressure needs to be reduced, or the room requires more general cooling.

The following figure shows a suggested perforated tile placement to cool racks with a front-to-back cooling model.

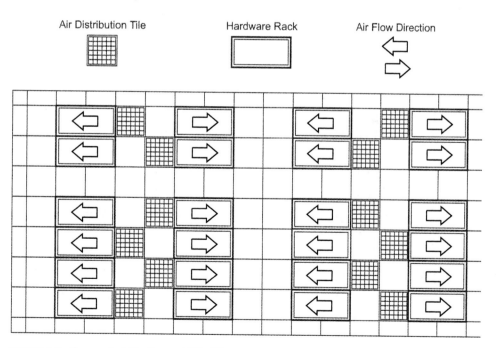

FIGURE 6-7 Suggested Perforated Tile Placement

Pressure Leak Detection

It is important to maintain pressure under the floor and allow air flow only through perforated tiles in the specific areas where it is needed. This will help to maximize the efficiency of the HVAC systems. However, rooms are not always perfectly square nor level, so voids in the raised floor, especially near walls and around pipes and conduits, occur. These voids allow air to escape from the floor void and decrease pressure.

The raised floor should be inspected routinely and any voids should be filled. Also, the perforated tiles that were used to direct air to machines that have been moved to a different location should be replaced with solid tiles. Replacing perforated tiles with solid tiles should be part of the standard procedure when a machine is removed or relocated.

Fire Rating

The raised floor system should be in compliance with the specifications laid out in the National Fire Protection Association document, *NFPA 75: Protection of Electronic/ Data Processing Equipment within the USA*, or relevant national standards outside the USA.

Local Building Code

Local building code could have something to say about how you implement the raised floor. This might be how many tile pullers (the device used to lift tiles) you need for the size of your raised floor. Or, inspectors could question the power distribution. For more information, see the section on PDUs in Chapter 7, "Power Distribution."

CHAPTER 7

Power Distribution

"Gimme gimme shock treatment."

- The Ramones

The power distribution system is the system that includes the main power feed into the data center (or the building), the transformers, power distribution panels with circuit breakers, wiring, grounding system, power outlets, and any power generators, power supplies, or other devices that have to do with feeding power to the data center equipment.

This chapter contains the following sections:

- "Power Distribution System Design"
- "Grounding and Bonding"
- "Signal Reference Grid"
- "Input Power Quality"
- "Wiring and Cabling"
- "Electromagnetic Compatibility"
- "Electrostatic Discharge"
- "Site Power Analyses"

Power Distribution System Design

A well-designed electrical system for the data center ensures adequate and consistent power to the computer hardware and reduces the risk of failures at every point in the system. The system should include dedicated electrical distribution panels and enough redundancy to guarantee constant uptime. A well-designed electrical system will provide consistent power and minimize unscheduled outages. Equipment subjected to frequent power interruptions and fluctuations is susceptible to a higher component failure rate than equipment connected to a stable power source.

Electrical work and installations must comply with local, state, and national electrical codes.

Assessing Power Requirements

Usually, your electrical design firm will tell you how much power is coming into the building as DC (Direct Current) which is expressed by KVA (Kilo Volt Amps). The easiest way to express this is in watts. When using DC power, volts × amps = watts (V×A=W). For example, you might be told that there is 7500KVA and that 7000KVA is available to the data center. The other 500KVA is needed for the rest of the building for offices, copiers, lighting, smoke detectors, soda machines, etc.

You can use the rack location units (RLUs) you've determined for your design to calculate how much power you need for equipment. The RLU definitions should include not only servers and storage equipment, but also network equipment such as switches, routers, and terminal servers. Add to this the power requirements of your HVAC units, fire control systems, monitoring systems, card access readers, and overhead lighting systems.

From your RLU definitions, you know that you'll need 800 30Amp 208V L6-30R outlets to power all of your racks. However, most circuit breakers will trip when they reach 80 percent of their rated capacity (this is sometimes referred to as a 0.8 diversity factor). A 30Amp breaker will really only allow a maximum of 24Amps through it before it trips and shuts down the circuit. Each circuit can handle about 5000 watts (24 amps × 208 volts = 4992 Watts) or 5KVA so the worst case electrical draw per outlet is 5KVA × 800 outlets = 4000KVA. No problem, because this is well within the 7000KVA you have allocated. However, most of the watts that these racks consume go into producing heat, and it will take quite a bit more electricity (for HVAC) to remove that heat.

A good rule of thumb is to take your total equipment power and add 70 percent for the HVAC system. The electrical usage will vary depending on the system and climatic conditions. Your HVAC and electrical designers should be able to give you a more precise multiplier once the HVAC system specifics are known.

4000KVA × 1.7 = 6800KVA, and that is within the 7000KVA you have been allocated. So, now you know that you have a large enough power in-feed to meet your electrical requirements.

The previous example uses the maximum draw that the breaker can accommodate before it trips. Most racks will not draw the full 5KVA, and it is possible that they could draw considerably less. The example of watt usage for RLU-A in Chapter 4, "Determining Data Center Capacities" is 3611 watts. This works out to a diversity factor of .58 (30Amps × 208 volts × .58 = 3619.2 watts). If you are building a data center that will be filled with just RLU-A racks, you could use a .58 diversity factor. However, this would mean that your average watts per RLU could not exceed 3619 watts. If you need to use a diversity factor below .80, you should use the highest wattage definition from all of your RLUs to determine the diversity factor. Also you must consider that power requirements will go up over time, so adding in an extra 3 to 5 percent to the diversity factor will also provide some headroom for next generation products that you can't anticipate during the design stages.

Finally, consider all possible future modifications, upgrades, and changes in power needs. For example, installing 50Amp wiring when only 30Amp is currently needed might be worth the extra cost if it is likely, within a few years, that machines will be added that need 40 to 50Amp wiring. The initial cost could be insignificant compared to the cost of dismantling part of the data center to lay new wire.

Consider the following questions during the design process:

- Is a certain amount of power allocated for the data center?
- Will power sources be shared with areas outside the data center?
- Where will the power feeds come from?
    - Will redundant power (different circuits or grids) be available?
    - Historically, how often do multiple grids fail simultaneously?
    - If power availability or dependability is a problem, can a power generating plant be built?
- Will the data center need single-phase or three-phase power (or both)?
- If the existing site is wired with single-phase, can it be retrofitted for three-phase?
- If you intend to use single-phase, will you eventually need to upgrade to three-phase?
    - Can you use three-phase wire for single-phase outlets, then change circuit breakers and outlets later when three-phase is needed?
- Where will the transformers and power panels be located? Is there a separate space or room for this?
- Which RLUs and their quantities need two independent power sources for redundancy?
- Will there be UPS? Where will the equipment be located?
- If there is only one external power feed, can half the power go to a UPS?
- Can a UPS be connected only to mission-critical equipment?

Multiple Utility Feeds

The availability profile of the data center could be the determining factor in calculating power redundancy. Ideally, multiple utility feeds should be provided from separate substations or power grids to ensure constant system uptime. However, those designing the center must determine whether the added cost of this redundancy is necessary for the role of the data center. It will be related to the cost of downtime and whatever other power delivery precautions you are taking. If you have a requirement for your own power generation as backup for data center power, then the additional costs of multiple utility feeds might not be cost effective. You should get historical data from your power supplier on the durations of outages in your area. This can be valuable information when making these decisions.

Uninterruptible Power Supply

An Uninterruptible Power Supply (UPS) is a critical component of a highly-available data center. In the event that power from the grid should fail, the UPS should be able to power 100 percent of the hardware for at least the amount of time needed to transfer power from an alternative utility feed or from backup generators. It should also be able to carry 150 percent of the power load to accommodate fault overload conditions. Don't forget to factor in the minimum HVAC power requirements. Also, include the power requirements needed for emergency lighting and any electronic equipment needed to access the data center, such as access card readers.

FIGURE 7-1 Control Panel and Digital Display of a UPS System

You might size your UPS to accommodate the actual power draw rather than the total power draw. For example, a machine might use 1500 watts for "normal" load. However, when it's powered on, it might initially draw 2200 watts. This load of 2200 watts is the "peak" load. You should size the UPS to handle this peak load.

However, this means a larger and more costly UPS. If budget is an issue, you will be taking a risk if you use a UPS rated for your normal load as it might fail to meet the peak load.

The UPS should be continually online, used to filter, condition, and regulate the power. Battery backup should be capable of maintaining the critical load of the room for a minimum of 15 minutes during a power failure to allow for the transfer of power from the alternate source, or to bring machines down cleanly if an alternate power source is not available. If a UPS is not used, surge suppression should be designed into the panels and a stand-alone isolation/regulation transformer should be designed into the power system to control the incoming power and protect the equipment.

Backup Power Generators

Backup power generators should be able to carry the load of the computer equipment, as well as all support equipment such as HVACs and network equipment. Depending on the availability status of the data center, it might be acceptable to use the UPS and multiple utility feeds without generators. If, by researching the power supply history, you determine that outages of 15 minutes or less are likely, you should install a UPS system with 20 minutes of battery power. This will sustain the data center until power is back on. If there is an outage of longer than 20 minutes, the data center will go down. This decision must be based on risk exposure determinations. The probability of a 20-minute outage might not outweigh the cost of generators.

If you plan for the use of generators, you'll need to think about code compliance, where they will be located (they give off exhaust), where the fuel tanks will be placed (one company used the same size tank used in gas stations, and it had to be buried), whether or not additional concrete pads must be installed, etc. You must also consider contracts with diesel suppliers.

Sharing Breakers

Though it is sometimes a necessary evil, sharing breakers is not recommended. As described in the earlier sections, machines don't use all of the capacity of their resident circuits. You have a normal load and a peak load. Two machines, each with a normal load of 1500 watts and a peak load of 2200 watts, could share the same 5KVA 30Amp circuit. However, if the configuration of these devices is changed over time, for example, if more memory is added, this might change the normal and peak loads, over the amount that the circuit could handle. While you might be forced to do this, you must be very careful and accurate in your power usage calculations for any circuit that you share.

FIGURE 7-2 Breaker Panel

Maintenance Bypass

The power system design should provide the means for bypassing and isolating any point of the system to allow for maintenance, repair, or modification without disrupting data center operations. The system should be designed to avoid all single points of failure.

Installation and Placement

The power distribution equipment for computer applications should be installed as close as possible to the load. All loads being supported must be identified and evaluated for compatibility with the computer equipment. Heavy loads that are cyclic, such as elevators, air conditioners, and large copy machines, should not be connected directly to the same source as the data center equipment.

Grounding and Bonding

Grounding is the creation of a path to an electrically conductive body, such as the earth, which maintains a zero potential (not positively or negatively charged) for connecting to an electrical circuit. This is usually done by connecting the data center equipment at the power source to an earth-grounding electrode subsystem which is a network of interconnected rods, plates, mats, or grids installed to establish a low-resistance contact with the earth. The purpose of the earth connection is to provide safety from shock to personnel and to protect the data center equipment from voltage gradients which could cause failures or fires. All metallic objects at the site that enclose electrical conductors or that are likely to be energized by electrical currents (for example, circuit faults, electrostatic discharge, or lightning) should be grounded for human safety, reducing fire hazards, protecting equipment, and to maintain optimal system performance.

A final reason for proper grounding is noise control, an important aspect of power quality.

Bonding is the means by which two or more grounding rods are connected. Proper bonding techniques are critical to proper grounding. You don't want to connect a grounding electrode to the central ground using a material that would act as an insulator, as this would add resistance to the path the electricity would take. The means by which you bond different grounding materials is specified by code. NFPA 70 1999, Article 250, sections 90 through 106, gives specific information on bonding. NFPA 70, section 250-90, defines bonding in general as "Bonding shall be provided where necessary to ensure electrical continuity and the capacity to conduct safely any fault current likely to be imposed."

A solid and well-bonded grounding system will allow circuit breakers to perform correctly, and ensure that devices like surge protectors and power sequencers connected to grounded outlets have a safe path to ground if an overcurrent situation occurs. In areas where overcurrent situations are likely, you can ground the metal chassis of a rack to the grounding system.

The common point of grounding can be connected to any number of sources at the service entrance (main power feed), for example:

- Driven earth rod
- Buried grid
- Building steel
- Water pipes

Whatever the sources, the ground should be carried through the entire system from these sources. Ideally, the central point of grounding at the service entrance will be connected to redundant ground sources such as building steel, buried grid, and cold water piping. A single source sets up the potential for a broken ground. A water pipe might be disjointed. Building steel could accumulate resistance over several floors. By tying into multiple grounds, ground loops are avoided, disruptions are minimized, and redundancy is achieved.

A university on the eastern seaboard lost all power from a problem with poorly grounded generators on the main power line. In the postmortem, it was found that there really was a postmortem. A raccoon seeking warmth had climbed into the generator housing and shorted out the circuit, creating a grounding loop, and knocking out the power. When everything was finally back online, another raccoon climbed into the generator and self-immolated, taking the power with it. After that, chicken wire was installed around the generator.

Compliance With the NEC

All grounding design should comply with the National Electrical Code (NFPA 70 or NEC) unless superseded by other codes. Article 250 of NFPA 70 1999 " covers general requirements for grounding and bonding of electrical installations, and specific requirements in (1) through (6).

1. Systems, circuits, and equipment required, permitted, or not permitted to be grounded.

2. Circuit conductor to be grounded on grounded systems.

3. Location of grounding connections.

4. Types and sizes of grounding and bonding conductors and electrodes.

5. Methods of grounding and bonding.

6. Conditions under which guards, isolation, or insulation may be substituted for grounding."

NFPA 70 1999 in section 250-2 (d) "Performance of Fault Current Path" states:

- **"...shall be permanent and electrically continuous."** The ground should be continuous from the central grounding point at the origin of the building system. If the path is installed in such a way that damage, corrosion, loosening, etc. could impair the continuity, then shock and fire hazards can develop. The ground should be dedicated and continuous for the whole system to avoid a ground differential that can occur from using various grounds.

- **"...shall be capable of safely carrying the maximum fault likely to be imposed on it."** Fault currents can be many times normal currents, and such high currents can melt or burn metal at points of poor conductivity. These high temperatures can be a hazard in themselves, and they can destroy the continuity of the ground-fault path.

- **"...shall have sufficiently low impedance to facilitate the operation of overcurrent devices under fault conditions."** A properly designed system will have as low an impedance as possible. If the ground-fault path has a high impedance, there will be hazardous voltages whenever fault currents attempt to flow. Also, if the impedance is high, the fault current will be limited to some value so low that the fuse or circuit breaker will not operate promptly, if at all.
- **"The earth shall not be used as the sole equipment grounding conductor or fault current path."** You have to use circuit breakers and valid grounding systems. You can't just rely on the fact that the building is connected to earth as the sole means of grounding.

NFPA 70 1999 Section 250-50 state that each of the items below "...shall be bonded together to form the grounding electrode system."

- Metal underground water pipe
- Metal frame of the building, where effectively grounded
- Concrete-encased electrode
- Ground ring

Furthermore, if metal underground water pipe is used, "continuity of the grounding path or the bonding connection to interior piping shall not rely on water meters or filtering devices and similar equipment." Additionally, a supplemental electrode is required.

NFPA 70 1999 section 250-52 states that if none of the previous grounding items are available, then, and only then, should you use the following:

- Other local metal underground systems or structures
- Rod and pipe electrodes
- Plate electrodes

The material in this section is reprinted with permission from NFPA 70, The National Electrical Code® Copyright ©1999, National Fire Protection Association, Quincy, MA 02269. This reprinted material is not the complete and official position of the National Fire Protection Association on the referenced subject, which is represented only by the standard in its entirety.

Equipment Grounding Conductor Impedance

The data center must have its own grounding plan which will tie into the earth ground for the rest of the building. The system should have sufficiently low resistance to allow circuit breakers, surge protectors, and power sequencers to respond to this overcurrent state very quickly. This resistance should be in the 1 to 5 ohm range. In the U.S., a 25-ohm maximum resistance value is the minimum standard for most "normal" grounding systems, according to the NEC. While this level of resistance is acceptable in a normal office environment, data centers should use the 5 ohms of resistance as the acceptable maximum resistance level for their grounding system.

The NEC and local codes require electronic equipment to be grounded through the equipment grounding conductor and bonded to the grounding electrode system at the power source. The impedance of the equipment grounding conductor from the electronic equipment back to the source neutral-ground bonding point is a measure of the quality of the fault return path. Poor quality connections in the grounding system will give a high impedance measurement. Properly installed equipment grounding conductors will give very low impedance levels. Equipment grounding conductors should have levels meeting code requirements with a value of less than 0.25 ohm.

Signal Reference Grid

A Signal Reference Grid (SRG) is a means to reduce high-frequency impedance (also called noise) so that a device or outlet has the lowest impedance path to earth ground. This grid has multiple paths to ground to ensure that grounding loops do not develop.

The SRG should be designed for the data center. This provides an equal potential plane of reference over a broad band of frequencies through the use of a network of low-impedance conductors installed throughout the facility. The following figure shows part of an SRG in a blueprint detail.

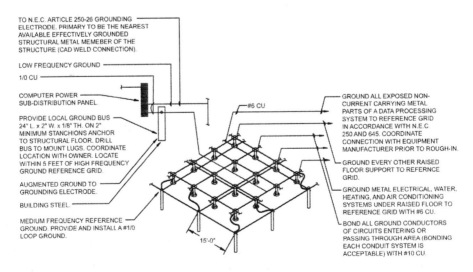

FIGURE 7-3 Blueprint Plan of a Signal Reference Grid

Recommended Practices

The following is a list of recommended practices for an SRG. This information should be well understood by the electrical engineer/contractor but should be used only as a reference because electrical codes in your area might be subject to different requirements.

1. **Follow applicable codes and standards for safe grounding.**

   There is no conflict between safe grounding for people and effective high-frequency grounding for sensitive electronic equipment.

2. **Install equipment ground bus.**

   Use sized 10" long, 1/4" thick, 4" high on 4" insulators. Bond via exothermic weld with #2 AWG bare copper to grounding ring.

3. **Provide exothermic weld or other code compiant connection between intersecting ground grid connectors.**

4. **Provide grounding/bonding for raised floor pedestal system in data center as follows:**

   Install #4 AWG bare copper for MFG (raised floor pedestal) grid. Bond to every other raised floor pedestal.

5. **Route #3/0 from equipment grounding bus bar to grounding bus bar in main electrical room.**

   Make sure that you have a path to earth ground.

6. **Bond HVAC units to perimeter ground or medium frequency ground loop via #6CU conductor.**

7. **Keep data and power cables on or near SRG.**

   All data and power cables should lay on or be very close to the SRG.

8. **Complete documentation.**

   Documentation should be complete in all details, including the proper grounding and bonding of heating, ventilation, and air-conditioning equipment, piping, raceways, and similar items. The responsible engineer should not expect the installers to complete the design.

Input Power Quality

The plans for the data center should include a well-designed power and grounding system to maintain appropriate conditions and avoid unplanned power outages. Numerous factors can disrupt, degrade, or destroy electronic systems. High-frequency, high amplitude noise, high ground currents, low power, surges and sags in voltage, harmonic distortion, and other factors will affect the proper functioning of equipment. It is essential that power conditioning technology be used to protect the data center equipment.

The following table shows a chart that was published by the U.S. Government as a Federal Information Processing Standard or FIPS. The source is FIPS PUB 94, "Guideline On Electrical Power for ADP Installations." The U. S. Government withdrew this standard July 29, 1997 because these tolerances or tighter tolerances had been adopted as industry standards. It is presented here only as a reference.

TABLE 7-1   FIPS PUB 94 Tolerances Chart

| Environmental Attribute | Typical Environment | Typical Acceptable Limits for Computers and Power Sources | | Units Affected and Comments |
		Normal	Critical	
Line frequency	0.1% - 3%	1%	0.3%	Disk packs, tape, regulators
Rate of frequency change	0.5-20 Hz/s	1.5 Hz/s	0.3 Hz/s	Disk packs
Over- and under-voltage	5-6%, -13.3%	+5%, -10%	3%	Unregulated power supplies
Phase imbalance	2%-10%	5% max	3% max	Polyphase rectifiers, motors
Power source: tolerance to low power factor	0.85-0.6 lagging	0.8 lagging	<0.6 lagging or 0.9 leading	Indirectly limits power source or requires greater capacity unit with reduced overall efficiency
Tolerance to high steady state peak current	1.3-1.6 peak/rms	1.0-2.5 peak/rms	>2.5 peak/rms	1.414 normal; departures cause wave shape distortion
Harmonics (voltage)	0-20% total rms	10-20% total; 5-10% largest	5% max total 3% largest	Voltage regulators, signal circuits

TABLE 7-1   FIPS PUB 94 Tolerances Chart *(Continued)*

Environmental Attribute	Typical Environment	Typical Acceptable Limits for Computers and Power Sources		Units Affected and Comments
		Normal	Critical	
DC load current capability of power source	Negligible to 5% or more	<0.1% w/ exceptions	As low as 0.5%	Half wave rectifier load can saturate some power source, trip circuits
Voltage deviation from sine wave	5-50%	5-10%	3-5%	Affects regulators, signal circuits
Voltage modulation	Negligible to 10%	3% max	1% max	Voltage regulators, servo motors
Transient surges/sags	+10%, -15%	+20%, -35%	+5%, -5%	Regulated power, motor torques
Transient impulses	2-3 times nominal peak value (0-130% V-s)	Varies: 1,000-1,500V typical	Varies: 200-500V typical	Memory, disks, tapes having data transfer rates, low level data signals
RFI/EMI and "tone bursts," normal and common modes	10V up to 20 Khz; less at high freq.	Varies widely-3V typical	Varies widely-0.3V typical	Same as above
Ground currents	0-10 A rms + impulse noise current	0.001-0.5 A or more	0.0035 A or less	Can trip GFI devices, violate code, introduce noise in signal circuits

Power Conditioning Technology

When the power source does not meet the equipment requirements, additional hardware might be required for power conditioning. These power conditioning systems can be separate or can be integrated into UPS equipment. The use of power conditioning systems is much like the use of UPS systems. A "power sag" or "brownout" is an event that can bring the delivery of power to under 80 percent of nominal power for a brief duration, usually two seconds or less, sometimes even in the milliseconds range. You can think of a power conditioning system as a three-to-five second UPS that will maintain the power flow through a brownout.

Harmonic Content

Harmonics problems can be caused by the interaction of data center equipment with the power loads or by switching power supplies. Harmonic distortion, load imbalance, high neutral current, and low power factor can result in decreases in equipment efficiency and reliability. Eliminating harmonics problems is difficult, because the computer hardware contributes to them, and any changes in the room load or configuration to fix the problem can create new problems.

Sun Microsystems equipment has been designed to address the problems of harmonic distortion and is generally compatible with similar modern equipment. Equipment that does not have the advantages of modern harmonic-correction features should be isolated on separate circuits.

Voltage Spikes

Voltage spikes are rises in the voltage caused most often within the power distribution circuits by components turning on and off, such as the cycling of compressor motors. Large spikes can interfere with energy transfer, or the associated electrical noise can cause signal corruption.

A UPS and/or filtering system will usually stop most spikes originating upstream of the UPS. If a UPS will not be installed, some other form of regulation or surge suppression should be designed into the system.

Lightning Protection

The potentially damaging effects of lightning on computer systems can be direct or indirect. It might be on the utility power feed, directly on the equipment, or through high-frequency electromagnetic interference or surge currents. Lightning surges cannot be stopped, but they can be diverted. The plans for the data center should be reviewed to identify any paths for surge entry, and surge arrestors that provide a path to ground should be included to provide protection against lightning damage. Protection should be placed on both the primary and secondary sides of the service transformer.

Lightning protection systems should be designed, installed, and maintained in accordance with NFPA 780 (1997 edition), *Standard for the Installation of Lightning Protection Systems*, or any superseding local or national code.

Emergency Power Control

NFPA 70 and NFPA 75 require a single point of disconnect for all electronic systems in the data center, at each point of entry. Multiple disconnects are also acceptable, but in either case, the switches must be unobstructed and clearly marked, as shown in the following figure.

FIGURE 7-4 Emergency Power Disconnect and Manual Fire Alarm Pull Station

Protective covers can be placed over the buttons to avoid accidental contact, but access cannot be locked out. The switch, or switches, should disconnect power to all computer systems, HVAC, UPS, and batteries. If the UPS is located within the data center, the disconnect should stop power to the unit. If the UPS is located remotely, the disconnect should stop the supply from the unit into the room.

Though not required by code, it is recommended that all power sources in the room be controlled by the disconnect to provide the highest degree of safety to personnel and equipment.

Wiring and Cabling

All wiring and cabling should be designed and installed in accordance with NFPA 70 of the National Electrical Code, or superseding national or local codes. All wiring and cabling should be run in an orderly and efficient manner, not like the "spaghetti" shown in the following figure.

FIGURE 7-5 Disorganized Cabling Under Floor Tiles

Data centers undergo frequent modifications, so any obsolete cabling should be removed to avoid air flow obstructions and minimize confusion and possible disconnection of the wrong cables during modification.

Note – Temporary extension cords should not be used in the subfloor void. If used above the raised floor, precautions should be taken to ensure that they don't pose a tripping hazard, and that they are not damaged.

Higher Amps and Single-Phase or Three-Phase

The main power feeds that enter a building are usually three-phase. Devices called transformers take the three phases of that power and convert them to three separate single phases. However, some computer equipment and support equipment runs on three-phase power only. Single-phase and three-phase power use different outlets, wiring, and circuit breakers. Use RLU definitions (see Chapter 4, "Determining Data Center Capacities") to determine how much single- and three-phase power you will need.

However, flexibility is an important part of design methodology, and we know that technology changes. It is possible that computer and network equipment suppliers will need to move larger systems to the use of three-phase power or higher amperage. Some already offer three-phase power as an option. So how can you design flexibility into your power system? One way is to gauge up your wiring requirements (pardon the pun).

Consider this scenario: Currently all of your RLU definitions use only single-phase power, L6-30R 30 Amp outlets. If you were to use the standard wire gauge for these outlets it will be fine. You can reuse this wire if you move to a three-phase outlet, provided that it still uses 30 Amps. However, if you were to use a standard wire gauge for 50 Amps, then this wire gauge would meet or exceed code requirements for the L6-30R 30 Amp outlets. Basically, you can use a larger gauge wire than is standard, but, not a smaller gauge wire. If you think you will need to change or upgrade power in the future, putting in the larger gauge wire for future use is a good idea. With this larger gauge wire in place, if you need to change some outlets to run at a higher amperage, you already have the wire ready and waiting under the floor.

Redistributing outlets from single-phase to three-phase is simple if the three-phase outlets run at the same amperage as the single-phase outlets they replace. For example: If you had three L6-30R single phase outlets each on their own circuit breaker, you could move to three-phase outlets of the same voltage by replacing only the outlets and swapping three of these single-phase circuit breakers for two three-phase breakers.

The following figure shows a section of electrical wireway for supporting the electrical requirements of two RLU Superset-A and one RLU-C.

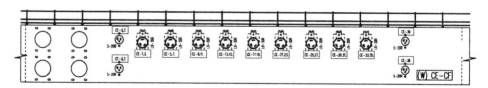

FIGURE 7-6   Blueprint Plan of a Standard Electrical Wireway and Outlets Under the Raised Floor

The wire gauge in the wireway can also support three-phase power as well as the current single-phase L6-30R existing outlets, since they are both running at 30 Amps. You can see four cutouts on the left side. These are already in the wireway so that, should three-phase power be needed later, six of the L6-30R outlets can be removed and the wiring used for four three-phase outlets. You can also see the labels for each outlet's circuit breaker. Six of these breakers can be removed at the sub-panel and replaced by four three-phase breakers.

There is another way to solve this problem: Power Distribution Units (PDUs).

Power Distribution Units

Historically, there was one or more power feeds into the building, and these power feeds fed transformers that would send portions of this electricity to sub-panels. These sub-panels contained the circuit breakers for each outlet on the floor. Wire for each outlet ran from the breakers out to the floor and terminated in an outlet. This is still is a fine system. However, if you need to change the outlet on the floor, you must change the breaker, the wire from the breaker out to the floor, and the outlet itself. In an operational data center, this is a difficult and time-consuming process. To run new wire out to the location on the floor means removing tiles in the raised floor. This leads to decreased pressure that can affect the proper cooling of operational equipment. While you could have flexibility in this system, it comes at a large cost to the smooth running of a working data center.

A Power Distribution Unit (PDU) is a way to integrate the circuit breakers, wire, and outlets in a central location on the floor that can service one or more RLUs. In this example, a PDU has an in-feed of 100A three-phase power by way of a Hubble connector. This Hubble connector plugs into the PDU. Inside the PDU is a smaller version of a sub-panel with circuit breakers for each outlet in the PDU. These circuit breakers have wires which connect to the individual outlets in the PDU. A PDU being fed by a 100Amp three-phase Hubble connector could supply eight 30Amp single-phase circuits. Another might supply ten 20Amp single-phase circuits, and another might supply four three-phase 30Amp outlets.

This gives a lot of flexibility in your electrical system. However, there are a few downsides to this design. The first concern is that it might not meet code. In the U.S., for example, the NEC is interpreted by local building authorities and can be superseded by other local electrical code. There are data centers in San Diego, California and Austin, Texas where PDUs under raised floors are acceptable to the local electrical code requirements. However, in Hillsboro, Oregon and Menlo Park, California, the use of PDUs under the raised floor are not acceptable under the local electrical code. Different states and different counties might have different interpretations of electrical code requirements.

The following figure shows an example of a PDU.

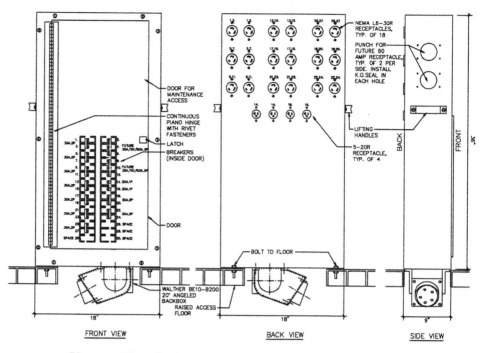

FIGURE 7-7 Blueprint Plan of a Power Distribution Unit

The other downside to the PDU design is availability. Currently, PDUs are custom-made devices and can be subject to lead times of weeks or months to manufacture. This is not a problem if you have a lot of lead time before you make changes to your electrical outlets. However, in the real world, this luxury isn't always available. With foresight, PDUs of whatever type you anticipate the need for can be pre-manufactured, but this involves additional cost for the materials (box, circuit breakers, wiring, and outlets) and labor to make, and the additional cost of storing them.

PDUs can offer a great deal of flexibility to your electrical design. However, your first requirement will be to find out if they will be acceptable to your local code requirements. And even if they are, they might not be the most cost effective model for your data center.

Electromagnetic Compatibility

Electromagnetic interference (EMI) and radio frequency interference (RFI) is radiated and conducted energy from electrical devices that produce electromagnetic fields. The electrical noise currents associated with these can interfere with the signals carried by the electronic components and the cabling of equipment.

Sources of EMI and RFI can be inside or outside the data center environment. Common external sources are airports, telecommunications or satellite centers, and similar facilities. Internal sources include the hardware itself. Sun equipment is tolerant of most common EMI/RFI levels. If high levels are suspected, a study should be conducted to determine whether shielding or other remedial actions are necessary.

Electrostatic Discharge

Electrostatic discharge (ESD) is the rapid discharge of static electricity between bodies at different electrical potentials and can damage electronic components. ESD can change the electrical characteristics of a semiconductor device, degrading or destroying it. It might also upset the normal operation of an electronic system, causing equipment to malfunction or fail.

Today's equipment has a much denser geometry, with thinner, more easily damaged materials. Though changes in design, manufacturing processes, and materials have reduced ESD sensitivity, components can still be damaged if precautions are not taken in the design of the data center and in component handling techniques. The damage can result in catastrophic failures, or it might not cause outright failure, but might make a component more susceptible to failure later on. Low grade failures due to cumulative degradation of components can be subtle and difficult to detect.

There are numerous ways to control static generation and ESD. The following list describes some of the control techniques.

- Since static electricity is a greater problem in an environment with low relative humidity (RH) levels, maintain appropriate relative humidity levels. This will help to dissipate charges.
- Limit or isolate the use of hardware that generates static charges.
- Limit or isolate activities and materials that generate static charges.
- Use only appropriate carts and furniture in the room.
- Don't use carpeted tiles!

- Operators should use appropriate personal grounding equipment such as anti-static lab coats, wrist straps, and heel grounders.

- Never use paper clips to press reset buttons! A good idea is to tape a few wooden toothpicks to the inside of the rack doors for use as reset button depressors.

- Keep covers on equipment racks closed. Covers should be opened only by trained personnel using proper grounding when inspections, repairs, or reconfigurations are necessary.

- The raised floor system should be properly grounded with static dissipative tile surfaces to provide a proper path to ground.

- Use only appropriate cleaning agents on floor tiles to maintain the static dissipative properties of the floor.

Site Power Analyses

Power disturbances can have numerous effects on sensitive electronic equipment, including data errors, system halts, memory or program loss, and equipment failures. Since it is often difficult to determine whether these problems are caused by power disturbances or by unrelated electronic equipment or software failures, a power system survey and analysis could be required. The analysis should be performed by professionals and should determine, at minimum, the following:

- The soundness of the power distribution (wiring) and grounding systems supplying power to the equipment

- The quality of the AC voltage supplying power to the equipment

- The source of power system disturbances

- The impact of power disturbances on data center equipment

The site power survey data should then be thoroughly examined to identify cost-effective improvements or corrections, both immediate and for the future.

CHAPTER 8

HVAC and Other Environmental Controls

"So hot you're cool, so cool you're hot."

- General Public

The control and maintenance of heating, ventilation, and air conditioning (HVAC), as well as relative humidity (RH) levels, is essential in the data center. Computer hardware requires a balanced and appropriate environment for continuous system operation. Temperatures and relative humidity levels outside of the specified operating ranges, or extreme swings in conditions, can lead to unreliable components or system failures. Control of these environmental factors also has an effect on the control of electrostatic discharge and corrosion of system components.

This chapter contains the following sections:

- "Reasons for Environmental Control"
- "Temperature Requirements"
- "Relative Humidity"
- "Electrostatic Discharge"
- "Air Conditioning Systems"
- "Humidification Systems"
- "Monitoring Temperature and RH Levels"
- "Mechanical Support Systems"
- "Air Distribution"

Reasons for Environmental Control

Computer rooms require precise and adaptable temperature control for several reasons:

- **Need for cooling.** Data centers have a dense heat load, generally 10 to 30 times the heat density of normal offices.

- **Cooling must be delivered where needed.** The heat load varies across the area of the computer room. To achieve a balanced psychrometric profile, the air conditioning system must address the needs of particular heat-producing equipment.

- **Data centers need precise cooling.** Electronic equipment radiates a drier heat than the human body. Therefore, precision data center cooling systems require a higher sensible heat ratio (SHR) than office areas. Ideally, the cooling system should have an SHR of 1:1 (100 percent sensible cooling). Most precision systems have sensible cooling between 85 and 100 percent, while comfort systems normally rate much lower.

- **Controls must be adaptable to changes.** The data center heat load will change with the addition or reconfiguration of hardware. Also, exterior temperature and humidity can vary widely in many places around the world. Both of these conditions will affect cooling capacities. Data center air conditioning systems must be chosen for their ability to adapt to these changes.

- **Data centers need frequent air exchange.** To create a precision cooling environment, the air must be exchanged at an adequate rate. While a normal office environment requires only two air changes per hour, the high-density heat load in a data center requires as many as 50 changes per hour. Precision air conditioners pass more than 500 cubic feet per minute (CFM) per ton, while comfort cooling air conditions might pass as little as 350 CFM per ton. If not enough air is exchanged in a given time, the cooling air will heat up before reaching the equipment it is meant to cool, and problems could occur.

Temperature Requirements

In general, an ambient temperature range in the data center of 70 to 74 F (21 to 23 C) is optimal for system reliability and operator comfort. Most computer equipment can operate within a wide psychrometric range, but a temperature level near 72 F (22 C) is best because it is easier to maintain safe associated relative humidity levels. Standards for individual manufacturers and components vary, so check the manufacturer's specifications for appropriate temperature ranges.

Another reason for keeping the temperature ranges maintained as close to the optimal temperature as possible is to give the greatest buffer against problems and activities that can change the temperature profile. Following are some possible causes of a change in the temperature profile:

- Component failure (or even scheduled maintenance) of the environmental support equipment
- Failure of any part of the HVAC or support systems
- Installations, deinstallations, or reconfigurations of hardware
- Removal of floor tiles for subfloor work, such as cabling
- Doors left open

With the center kept at the optimal temperature, these influences have less of an overall effect on equipment.

Relative Humidity

Relative humidity (RH) is the amount of moisture in a given sample of air at a given temperature in relation to the maximum amount of moisture that the sample could contain at the same temperature. If the air is holding all the moisture it can for a specific set of conditions, it is said to be saturated (100 percent RH). Since air is a gas, it expands as it is heated, and as it gets warmer the amount of moisture it can hold increases, causing its relative humidity to decrease. Therefore, in a system using subfloor air distribution, the ambient relative humidity will always be lower than in the subfloor.

Ambient levels between 45 and 50 percent RH are optimal for system reliability. Most data processing equipment can operate within a fairly wide RH range (20 to 80 percent), but the 45 to 50 percent range is preferred for several reasons:

- **Corrosion.** High humidity levels can cause condensation within computer equipment which can cause corrosion to components. For more information, refer to "Corrosion" on page 103.

- **Electrostatic Discharge (ESD).** ESD can cause intermittent interference in equipment. It is easily generated and less easily dissipated when the RH is below 35 percent and becomes critical at lower ranges. For more information, refer to "Electrostatic Discharge" on page 103.

- **Operating time buffer.** This humidity range provides the longest operating time buffer in the event of environmental control system failure.

Although the temperature and humidity ranges for most hardware are wide, conditions should always be maintained near the optimal levels. The reliability and the life expectancy of the data center equipment can be enhanced by keeping RH levels within the optimal ranges.

Certain extremes (swings) within this range can be damaging to equipment. If, for example, very high temperatures are maintained along with very high percentages of RH, moisture condensation can occur. Or, if very low temperatures are maintained along with very low percentages of RH, even a slight rise in temperature can lead to unacceptably low RH levels.

The following table shows ranges for temperatures, relative humidity, and altitude.

TABLE 8-1   Environmental Requirements

Environmental Factor	Optimal	Operating	Non-Operating
Temperature	70 to 74 F (21 to 23 C)	50 to 90 F (10 to 32 C)	-4 to 140 F (-20 to 60 C)
Relative humidity	45% to 50% RH	20% to 80% RH (noncondensing)	Up to 93% RH
Altitude	Up to 10,000 ft (3,048 m)	Up to 10,000 ft (3,048 m)	Up to 40,000 ft (12,192 m)

Note – Severe temperature or RH swings should be avoided. Conditions should not be allowed to change by more than 10 F (5.5 C) or 10 percent RH in any 60-minute period of operation.

Corrosion

Excessive humidity in the air increases the corrosive potential of gases and should be avoided in the data center environment. Gases can be carried in the moisture in the air and transferred to equipment in the data center.

Drastic temperature changes should also be avoided. These can cause latent heat changes leading to the formation of condensation. This usually happens in areas where hot and cold air meet, and this can cause a number of hardware problems.

- Water can react with metals to form corrosion.
- Water can electrochemically form conductive solutions and cause short circuits.
- If there are electrical potential differences between two dissimilar metals in a component, electrolytic or galvanic corrosion can occur.
- Water can form a reactive combination with gases present in the air, and the resultant compounds can corrode hardware.

Keep relative humidity levels at the appropriate percentage.

Electrostatic Discharge

Electrostatic discharge (ESD) is the rapid discharge of static electricity between bodies at different electrical potentials and can damage electronic components. ESD can change the electrical characteristics of a semiconductor device, degrading or destroying it. It might also upset the normal operation of an electronic system, causing equipment to malfunction or fail.

For more information on ESD, see page 96.

Air Conditioning Systems

In the simplest terms, HVAC units are really big air conditioners, not dissimilar to the air conditioning unit in your car, apartment, or house.

The efficiency of a precision air conditioning system is based on two things:

- The degree of temperature control
- The ability of the system to get the conditioned air to the units of hardware that need cooling

The following figure shows an HVAC unit and controls.

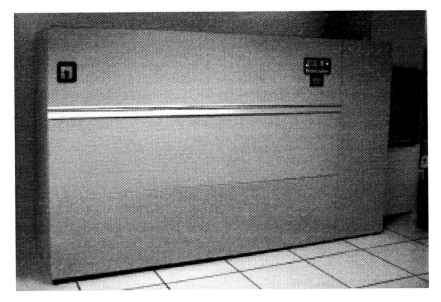

FIGURE 8-1   HVAC Unit

Chilled Liquid Systems

The basic premise of a chilled liquid system is that air goes into the unit through its intake (at the top of most HVAC units) and is passed through a set of filters, some of which are electrically charged to attract dust particles and other contaminants. Once filtered, the air passes through a series of coils that contain fluid at much lower temperature than the air. A heat exchange between the temperature of the air and the temperature of the fluid in these coils occurs, lowering the temperature of the air. The cooled air is passed out of the HVAC unit at higher speed and pressure with fans that force it into the supply plenum (usually the raised floor). HVAC units can also have humidifiers which add an atomized stream of water to the air. This changes the RH of the air to keep it at the appropriate level. The fluid in the coils is sent out of the unit to cooling towers to expel the heat.

The HVAC unit will have set points for both ideal temperature and humidity levels, like the thermostat in a house. Sensors located within the data center track both the temperature and humidity of the air. This information is fed back to the HVAC unit and the unit adjusts its heat transfer and the humidifier moisture level to meet its set points.

Dry Conditioning Systems

In areas that have high humidity, a dry conditioning system could be more appropriate than a chilled liquid system. A dry conditioning system uses a lithium chloride solution applied in a constant stream to a saturated cellulose honeycomb material. As outside air comes in contact with this lithium chloride solution, the water vapor in the air reacts with the solution. The solution absorbs humidity and generates heat, which cools and dehumidifies the air. This cooler and less humid air can then be sent to a secondary chilled liquid system. Since the air going into the chilled liquid system has already been partially cooled, less work and energy is expended to bring the air to the needed temperature and RH levels. Portions of the now heated lithium chloride solution are pumped through a filter system and heat exchanger. The heat exchanger drives a heat pump to assist in regenerating the lithium chloride solution, removing the heat and humidity, and prepare the solution to go through the process again.

Since this system relies on water vapor to create the chemical reaction and cool the air, it is only appropriate in areas where the ambient humidity in the outside air is well above the ideal 45 percent needed in a data center. Areas like Atlanta, Georgia and Tokyo, Japan, are better suited to this kind of HVAC "preprocessing." It would not be as useful in areas with very low ambient humidity like Las Vegas, Nevada, or Phoenix, Arizona.

Planning Air Circulation

Air flow planning is critical because it affects the placement of data center racks. The racks have two footprints, physical and cooling. The cooling footprint is what you need to know at this stage of the design. If you have racks that cool side to side, you will need more clearance than if they're cooled top to bottom. You can't place two side-cooling machines next to each other with zero side clearance. Also, if machines are cooled front-to-back, the use of a back-to-back cooling model, alternating hot and cool aisles, is critical.

Consider the air flow patterns of the storage and server equipment to be installed in the data center.

- Does it draw air directly from the subfloor?
- Does it draw air from the room?
- Is the heated air exhausted from the back or the top or the side of the rack?
- Does the air flow through the equipment from side-to-side, front-to-back, front-to-top, or bottom-to-top?
- Do all of the units in a rack have the same air flow patterns or are some different?

Since the equipment from different manufacturers can have different air flow patterns, you must be careful that the different units don't have conflicting patterns, for example, that the hot exhaust from one unit doesn't enter the intake of another unit. Sun equipment is usually cooled front-to-back or bottom-to-top. Bottom-to-top is the most efficient way to cool equipment, drawing directly from the supply plenum and exhausting to the return plenum in the ceiling. It also creates a more economical use of floor space since no open area to the sides of the equipment are needed for free cooling space.

For more about air flow in general, see Chapter 6, "Implementing a Raised Floor."

Downward Flow System

Optimally, an air conditioning system with a cold plenum low, return plenum high ("downward") flow should be used. For a small amount of hardware space, appropriate conditions can be maintained with other designs. However, the air flow patterns in the downward flow design allow for the most efficient hardware cooling.

These systems work by drawing air into the top of the HVAC unit, either from the room or from the return plenum (return air), where it is cleaned by air filter banks, and passed over a cooling coil. The conditioned air (supply air) is then pushed by large fans at the bottom of the unit into the plenum between the subfloor and raised floor. The forced air is directed into the computer space through cable cutouts, or perforated floor tiles. Once in the ambient room space, the conditioned air mixes with the hardware heat load by passing through the rack, absorbing heat, then flows back to the air conditioners through the return plenum for reconditioning. This produces an efficient air flow pattern using natural convection currents.

The downward flow air conditioning system used in data centers is typically incorporated with a raised floor system. The raised floor should be 24 inches (60 cm) above the subfloor to allow space to run network and power cables, and for the passage of air. The modular tile design makes it easy to reconfigure hardware and air distribution patterns. When hardware is added, solid and perforated tiles can be positioned to deliver conditioned air to the hardware intakes.

For more information on the raised floor system, see Chapter 6, "Implementing a Raised Floor."

Overhead Air Handlers

Overhead air introduction or upflow air conditioning should be avoided due to their associated turbulent air flow patterns. The following figure shows an example of the difference in efficiency between an upward and downward air flow system.

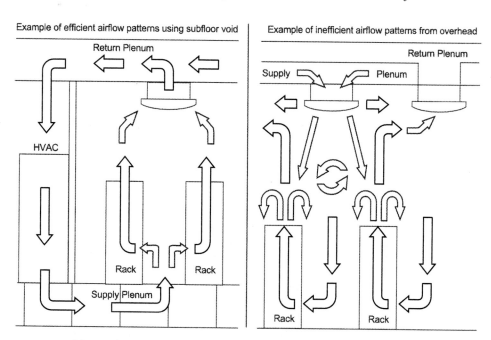

FIGURE 8-2 Upward vs. Downward Air Flow Patterns

The majority of the hardware in most data centers takes in air for cooling at the front or bottom of the unit and exhausts it out the back or top. Introducing conditioned air from the ceiling causes turbulence when the conditioned air meets the hot exhaust. A higher cooling load is needed to address this inefficiency.

Centralized Air Handling

Centralized systems, using a single large air handling unit, should be avoided. The problems with centralized systems are:

- Lack of the degree of control you will get with multiple units
- Lack of redundancy; when the central system is down, there is no HVAC

- In such systems, temperature and RH are regulated by a single sensor set in the ambient space of the room or the return air duct. It is unlikely that conditions in all areas of the room are the same as they are at this single sensor point, so an inaccurate presentation of room conditions will be given.

Placement of HVAC Units

HVAC units are placed depending on your heat load criteria, and this is one of the reasons that cooling is part of the RLU specifications. If 25 percent of your data center will contain 50 percent of the heat load, then equally distributing your HVAC units around the data center would not be the most efficient use of your cooling capacity. Where they are placed depends on the capacity of each unit to cool and deliver the air to the correct locations on the floor. You should work with your HVAC engineers to determine the ideal placement of your HVAC units for maximum efficiency. While it is critical to work with all of your contract professionals, it is particularly important to work with knowledgeable HVAC engineers. In many areas there are little or no building code requirements for HVAC systems used in data centers.

If the room is a long thin rectangle, you can probably place the HVAC units along the perimeter of this room and get enough cold air volume to the center area. If the room is a large square, you can place units at the perimeter and down the center as well, creating in effect two long thin rectangles within the room. This creates zones of cold air at the required pressure for a given area to meet its cooling requirements.

Additionally, software for simulations of air flow and heat transfer is available. "Flovent" software from Flomerics uses Computational Fluid Dynamics (CFD) techniques to allow for HVAC simulation of data center environments. These models can include raised floor height, obstructions under the floor, placement and percentage of perforated tiles, servers, storage systems, and the placement of HVAC units.

Most HVAC systems require some liquid like water or coolant to exchange the heat from the air as it goes through the unit, and this liquid is moved outside of the room (and probably the building) to expel the heat it has absorbed. Pipes containing this liquid will be within, or quite close to, your data center. As you know, water and electricity are a nasty combination. If you put HVAC units on the floor, you must ensure that these pipes have troughs or channels to redirect the fluid out of the data center in the case of a pipe failure. One way to do this is to locate as many HVAC units as possible, perhaps all of them, outside the data center.

The following figure shows how the mechanical rooms that house the HVAC units are connected just on the outside of the walls for the data center.

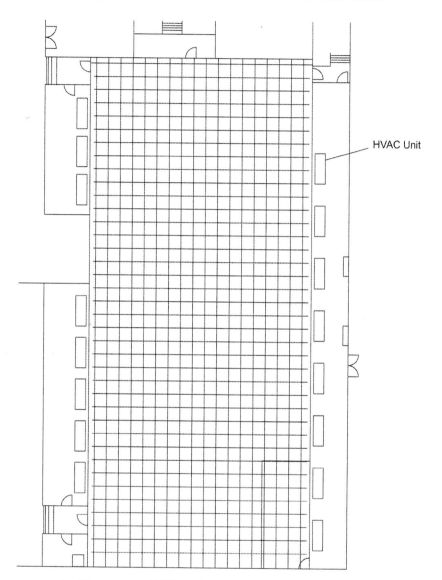

HVAC Unit

FIGURE 8-3   Placement of HVAC Units Outside the Data Center Room

All the pipes needed for these units can be located outside the data canter, as well. There should be a 4-inch barrier at the perimeter of the data center to prevent liquid from the pipes from entering the data center if a pipe were to fail. This also gives a clean access to the base of the HVAC unit to pump cold air under the floor with minimal obstruction. Since these units are outside the walls of the data center, the raised floor and dropped ceiling voids can be used as supply and return plenums, respectively.

Humidification Systems

Humidification can take place within the air conditioners, or by stand-alone units. In some data centers, it might be better to introduce moisture directly into the room where it will mix easily with the ambient temperatures. This can be done with individual humidifiers, separate from the HVAC units. These should be units designed to keep the psychrometric rates of change to a narrow margin, monitor the room conditions, and adapt to the current room and equipment demands. Separate units throughout the room increase the amount of control over humidification and offer redundancy.

HVAC units are available with the capability of adding moisture to the air flow, but they might not be the best solution due to the way they do this. Possible problems with introducing moisture directly to air within the HVAC units are:

- Cold air flows cannot accept high levels of moisture, so the moisture will condense.
- Condensation can form within the process coolers and cause corrosion, reducing the operational life of the units.
- Condensation can create water buildup and spills.
- HVAC units that introduce cooling air into the subfloor mix moisture with cold air that might be near saturation. This can cause condensation and corrosion within the subfloor system.

However, separate humidifier and HVAC systems will be more expensive than containing the humidifier in the HVAC unit itself. Separate units will also add to labor costs. The placement of RH systems out under the raised floor will require water, in either pipes or bottled form, to be within the data center so the same precautions must be taken as with pipes that are in the data center space. As you can see, there is no right answer. Each approach has its advantages and disadvantages. You must determine what is the correct solution for your data center.

A recommended humidification system, available as a separate unit or as part of an HVAC unit, uses a closed water bottle that contains electrodes to heat the contained water and produce steam. The closed bottle design removes any suspended contaminant particles from the supply water resulting in clean output. Also, ultrasonic humidifiers might be an effective choice.

Whatever system is chosen, carefully consider redundancy to ensure that the humidification needs of the room are met without serious disruption.

Monitoring Temperature and RH Levels

Because of the importance of both temperature and relative humidity in keeping the data center continually up and running, it is critical to keep a constant check on the temperature and RH levels. The data center system must provide constant feedback with a detailed profile of the room conditions.

Monitoring System

A comprehensive monitoring system is an added expense to the design and maintenance of the facility, but it provides an invaluable tool for diagnosing and correcting problems, collecting historical data for system evaluations, and for day-to-day verification of room conditions. The following should be considered in the design of the data center and monitoring system:

- The room condition feedback should not be based on one sensor in one part of the room. A single sensor might tell that conditions are perfect, but in truth, they are only perfect in that particular part of the room. Sensors should be placed in specific areas of the center and near critical configurations. These sensors usually sense both temperature and RH. You could have separate sensors for these, but they will also be connected to a data storage device, and simultaneous temperature and RH information read by a specific sensor is the information you want recorded.

- The monitoring system should have historical trend capabilities. The historical psychrometric data can be used to analyze seasonal changes and other outside influences.

- The monitoring system should have critical alarm capabilities. At the very least, the system should be set to notify when conditions move outside the set parameters. It might also be necessary to have a system that performs automatic functions such as switching to a backup chiller if a primary chiller fails.

- Ideally, the monitoring system should be integrated with a tracking system for all parts of the center. This would include not only the in-room air conditioners and humidifiers, but the cooling support systems, power backup, fire detection and suppression, water detection, security, and any other infrastructure and life-safety systems.

- The HVAC system configuration and monitoring data should be periodically examined and evaluated by trained personnel to ensure that temperature and RH profiles are appropriate for the current room demands.

- These monitoring systems can use SNMP protocol to integrate into overall data center management systems.

Air Conditioner and Humidifier Set-Points

The set-points of the environmental support equipment will vary between data center sites, and even between individual units in the same site. An advantage of multiple HVAC and humidifier units is the ability to modify set-points individually in localized areas. The heat load in a room will vary from an area with dense hardware configurations to an area with little or no hardware. Adjusting for this variance can be done by changing the tile configurations in the raised floor, but adjustments to the HVAC or humidifier set-points might also be necessary. Ideally, these settings would be monitored and adjusted from a single console.

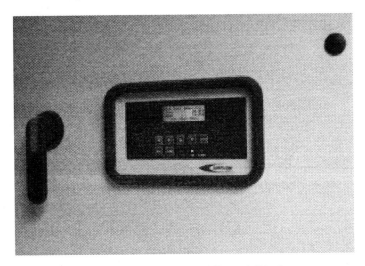

FIGURE 8-4 HVAC Control Panel and Digital Display

Under most circumstances:

- Air conditioners should be set to 72 F (22 C) with a sensitivity range of +/- 2 F (-16 C)
- Humidifiers should be set to 48 percent RH with a sensitivity range of +/- 3% RH

The decision for set-point settings will be influenced by several factors, including heat load and vapor barrier integrity. If, for example, the room has inadequate vapor barriers, it might be necessary to adjust humidifier set-points to accommodate seasonal influences.

The set-points should be chosen to maintain the optimal recommended temperature and RH levels while allowing wide enough sensitivity ranges to avoid frequent cycling of the units.

Mechanical Support Systems

In general, equipment produces heat which warms up the room beyond acceptable operating temperatures, so the work of the support systems is to move cool air in to cool the machines, and to move hot air out. Sometimes the hot air is recycled, cooled, and returned to cool the machines. Cooling systems for conditioning the air take different forms, but typically the designs use water or refrigerants.

The following figure shows two cooling towers awaiting installation.

FIGURE 8-5   Cooling Towers Waiting to be Connected to an HVAC System

When designing the data center, the support system must be taken into consideration. Design concerns include:

- **Adequate space.** There must be adequate space to house large equipment such as chillers, cooling towers, condensers, and the requisite piping system.

- **Climate.** The climate of the area might partially determine the types of systems used. For example, using cooling towers that rely on simple heat transfer to the outside air will be less efficient in Las Vegas than, say, Toronto, since the normal ambient air temperature is higher. Local codes might have restrictions on what types of systems you must use.

- **Flexibility.** If there are plans to expand the data center in the future, expansion of the support system should also be considered.

- **Redundancy.** There must be enough built-in redundancy so that the loss of any one component of the system will not significantly impact the system as a whole. The system should be designed to allow for repairs or upgrades while the center is online.

- **Minimize leaks.** The system should be designed to minimize leakage of water or refrigerants within the controlled area of the data center. Piping should not be run through the ceiling void. Air conditioner piping (the lines that carry the coolant) should not run directly in front of the HVAC unit's exhaust that sends the chilled air out into the supply plenum. Multiple taps should be installed into chilled water piping to simplify configuration changes. The best data center layout would keep all piping out of the data center. This would involve placing HVAC units outside the controlled area with a catch system in place to drain any liquids away from the center.

- **Monitor the system.** The mechanical support systems must be connected to the building monitoring system. Status and critical alarms must be recorded and reported to Maintenance and IT.

Air Distribution

If you think of the controlled environment of a data center as a cocoon, it's easier to imagine how forced currents of air are heated and cooled in a continuous cycle. The basic principle of convection is what makes the system work: Cold air drops, hot air rises.

The cycle of air flow in the room follows this basic pattern:

- Air is cooled as it passes through the air conditioning (HVAC) units.
- Conditioned air is forced into the raised floor void and directed up into the room and into equipment racks by means of tiles with perforations or cutouts.
- Conditioned air continues through equipment racks, cooling components.
- Heated air from components is forced out of the racks and rises toward the ceiling.
- Warm air is drawn back into the HVAC units where it is cooled and forced back into the raised floor to continue the cooling cycle.

Tile Placement and Air Flow

The modular design of the floor tiles that make up the equipment surface on a raised floor system are the building blocks for precise air distribution. The number and types of tiles necessary depend on specific characteristics of the site and the predetermined layout of the data center equipment. However, the following guidelines should be considered:

- **Number of perforated tiles.** Air conditioner manufacturers usually recommend a specific amount of opening in the floor surface in the form of air distribution tiles for each model of air conditioner they produce. The precise number of perforated tiles and where they will be placed must be determined by the location of heat-producing equipment. Floor tiles are typically 2 ft x 2 ft square. A typical 25 percent perforation tile represents one square foot of open area.

- **Tile placement.** Air distribution tiles should be positioned to deliver conditioned air to the intake of each rack. Solid tiles should be positioned to redirect air flow to the perforated tiles.

- **Subfloor pressure.** The subfloor pressure differential enables the efficient distribution of conditioned air. The pressure under the floor should be at least 5 percent greater than the pressure above the floor. Also, it might be necessary to adjust the number and position of perforated tiles to maintain appropriate pressure levels. It is the difference in pressure under the raised floor and above the raised floor that allows the cold air to flow correctly. Therefore, the pressure under the raised floor must be greater than the air pressure above the raised floor. You can use perforated tiles to modify this pressure change. Consider an example with two racks: The first, Rack A, is 20 feet from the HVAC unit. The second, Rack B, is 40 feet from the HVAC unit. The pressure under the floor at Rack A is x, and a 25 percent perforated tile provides an acceptable pressure differential to allow enough cold air to properly cool the machine. By the time the remaining air gets to Rack B, 20 feet further away, the pressure is $x/2$. To get the same amount of air to the machine when the air pressure is half, you need a 50 percent perforated tile, or two 25 percent perforated tiles right next to each other.

- **Avoid air leaks.** Unnecessary air leaks often occur through oversized cable cutouts or poorly cut partial tiles (against a wall, around a pillar, etc.). These breaches compromise the subfloor pressure and overall cooling efficiency. Fillers or protective trim should be fitted to these tiles to create a seal.

- **Avoid cooling short cycles.** Cooling short cycles occur when cold air from the air conditioner returns to the air conditioner before it has cycled through the heat-producing equipment. This happens when perforated tiles are placed between an air conditioner and the nearest unit of heat-producing hardware, as shown in FIGURE 8-6.

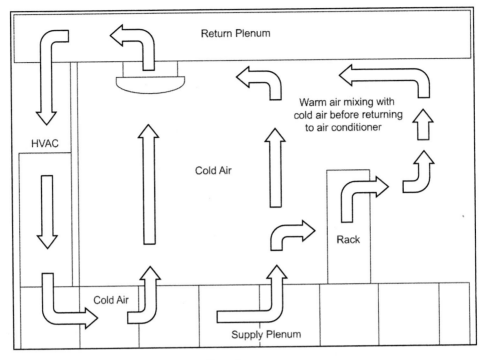

FIGURE 8-6 Cooling Short Cycle Air Flow Patterns

Since cool air is being cycled back to the air conditioner, the regulating sensors at the return air intake will register a cooler room condition than is accurate. This will make the unit cycle out of cooling mode while the cooling needs of the equipment have not been addressed. This affects both temperature and relative humidity.

■ **Avoid subfloor obstructions.** The subfloor is the path conditioned air travels to the machines, so everything should be done to minimize any obstructions in this path. In a perfect world, nothing should be in the subfloor but air. However, this is not always practical. Having power outlets and conduit above the subfloor will reduce obstructions, but it puts power cables in harm's way. The same is true with network cabling. However, you can take steps to reduce these obstructions. One way is to mount cable trays on the power conduit below the raised floor. Use cable trays that allow air to flow through them. If you are using patch panels on the floor or the POD design (see Chapter 9, "Network Cabling Infrastructure") you will have "home runs" of cables from areas on the floor back to the network room. Route these "home runs" through the ceiling rather than under the raised floor.

Hardware Rack Placement

The placement of hardware racks is dependent on several factors, including but not restricted to the following:

- Location of existing entryways and ramps
- Columns and other unavoidable obstructions
- Oddly shaped areas
- Aisles and other breaks in rack rows
- Available power connections
- Cooling requirements

The last item in the list is the most common restricting factor.

The heat load of small individual servers or storage arrays is generally low, but the density increases dramatically when the devices are stacked in racks. Also, newer technologies tend to condense the geometry of the electronics which thereby increase the density of the heat load. This is why it is important to determine the heat load based on RLUs (Chapter 4, "Determining Data Center Capacities").

The majority of Sun servers and storage arrays are designed to take in conditioned supply air at the front, pass it over the heat loads of the internal components, and exhaust it at the rear. Sun racks can house a wide variety of devices with differing air flow patterns. Some devices move air bottom to top, some from front to back, others from one side to the other.

The front-to-back air flow pattern suggests a front-to-front (and back-to-back) row and aisle configuration as shown in FIGURE 8-7. With this configuration, direct transfer of the hot exhaust from one rack into the intake of another rack is eliminated.

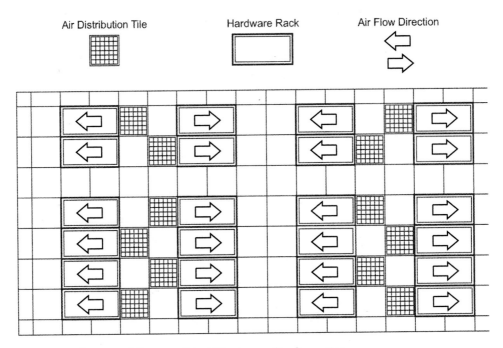

FIGURE 8-7 Suggested Front-to-Front Hardware Configuration

In this example, the aisle width is 4 feet (1.22 meters), and the side-to-side spacing is virtually zero. Enough clearance should be maintained to allow any rack in the lineup to be removed for service or replacement. Note the breaks in the rows to allow easy access between rows.

If, for some reason, the racks must be installed with the air flow going in the same direction, there must be adequate space between the aisles to avoid the direct transfer of hot exhaust from one rack into the intake of another rack, as shown in FIGURE 8-8.

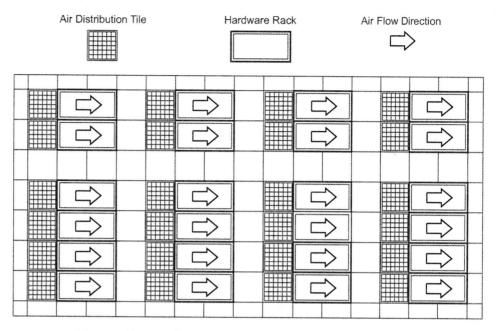

FIGURE 8-8 Alternate Front-to-Back Hardware Configuration

The amount of aisle space necessary will depend on the efficiency of the cooling system. If the cooling system and the possibilities for efficient air distribution are less than optimal, it might be necessary to increase the amount of aisle space, and possibly the space between the racks to spread out the heat load.

In terms of rack spacing, consider the following:

- Aisle widths might be different depending on the size of the racks. Both the standard Sun storage rack and the Sun Fire 6800 server rack are two feet by four feet and would require a minimum of four feet (1.2 m) of aisle space. These widths could be different depending on tile and cutout placement.

- There must be breaks within the equipment rows to allow operators access between rows and to the backs of the racks.

- The design of the equipment rows should be based on local fire regulations.

- The air conditioning returns should be placed so that the warm air from the equipment has a clear path into them. In the case of a low ceiling, this is problematic as the warm air must build up until it can be drawn into the air conditioner intakes. A much better design implements a dropped ceiling with vents to allow warm air to rise up into the return plenum. From there, the hot air can be drawn efficiently back to the HVAC units. FIGURE 8-9 shows an efficient method of cycling the warm air back to the HVAC units located outside the data center walls through a return plenum.

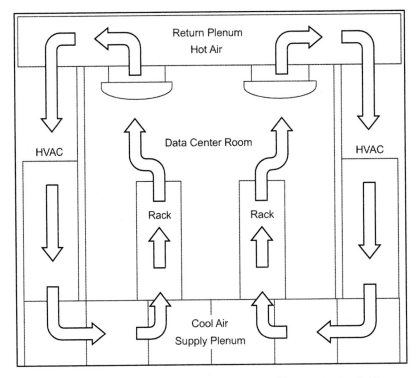

FIGURE 8-9 Cycling Warm Air Through a Return Plenum in the Ceiling

Subfloor Pressure Differential

When conditioned air is forced into the subfloor void (plenum) it meets with resistance of the contained area which creates the subfloor pressure. This pressure builds up unless the air can find a way to escape. Escape routes are designed into the floor tiles in the form of cutouts and perforations in specific percentages, acting to distribute the cool air to the equipment in the room. The pressure is critical to the functioning of the equipment cooling system, and the pressure and air flow destinations can be controlled. This control is based on the following factors:

- The amount of air forced into the plenum (number of HVAC units and velocity).

- The distance the air must travel to get to the equipment it is meant to cool.

- Where air distribution tiles are placed in the room. (See the section "Tile Placement and Air Flow" on page 115 for more details.)

- The percentage of perforation in the placed air distribution tiles. (See the section "Tile Placement and Air Flow" on page 115 for more details.)

- Other breaches in the supply plenum, such as cable cutouts or missing tiles. (See the following section, "Supply Air Plenum Integrity," for more details.)

The pressurization level must be adequate to move the right amount of cool air to the right parts of the data center. This pressure is regulated by the velocity of the air out of the HVAC units and the distribution and percentages of perforated tiles used.

The pressurization levels in the plenum should be regularly monitored. This is especially important when any subfloor work must be done, because removing floor tiles will degrade subfloor pressure. Each 2 ft ×2 ft solid tile represents 4 feet of floor area, equivalent to four perforated tiles with 25 percent perf. If many floor tiles must be removed for subfloor work, it might be necessary to compensate for lost pressure.

Supply Air Plenum Integrity

As emphasized in the previous section, the subfloor void in a downward-flow air conditioning system must be kept at an adequate pressure to properly cool equipment in the room above. The positive pressurization is created by initially introducing more air into the plenum than is allowed to escape into the data center room. To maintain the pressure and control the air flow, all breaches in the plenum must be intentional and part of the integrity of the air flow system. Unintentional breaches make planning the pressure levels difficult.

To maintain the integrity of the supply air plenum, avoid the following:

- **Too many air distribution tiles.** The number of perforated tiles should be carefully determined to maintain proper pressurization. A typical 25 percent perforation tile represents one foot of free area. Higher perforation percentage tiles should be used with caution, because they limit air distribution adjustment.

- **Oversized cutouts.** Custom cutouts in tiles are typically for cable passage, to fit around support columns, and for other oddly shaped corners. Partial tiles are sometimes created to fill in around perimeter walls. The number of cutouts should be limited and carefully made. Oversized cutouts should be fitted with appropriate sealing trim or filled with closed-cell foam.

- **Poor fitting tiles.** Only tiles that accurately fit the support grid should be used. Replace any tiles that allow air to escape around the edges. Loose fitting partial tiles along any perimeter walls should be replaced or fit with trim to seal the gaps.

- **Perimeter penetrations.** Check for holes in the subfloor perimeter walls. These could be passages for cabling, conduit, or pipes and can constitute major leaks. Fill them with appropriate materials such as closed-cell foam. Seal any cracks or joints in perimeter walls and subfloor deck. Do not use any materials that might hinder the functioning of expansion joints. Fix any gaps between the perimeter walls and the structural deck or roof.

- **Cable chases.** Cable chases in PODs and into adjacent rooms can compromise air pressure in the subfloor. Holes in columns that route cable between subfloor plenum and ceiling plenum are a concern. The columns can act as chimneys depleting subfloor pressure and pressurizing the ceiling void. A pressurized ceiling void creates convection problems, diminishing the efficiency of the cooling system.

- **Out-of-service HVAC units.** If an HVAC unit is turned off for an extended period of time, the output should be blocked with an appropriate, non-shedding material. Left unblocked, subfloor pressure will force itself back through the unit. This not only drains pressure from the plenum, but the reverse air flow through the unit can dislodge particulate contaminants from the filters and force them into the supply air.

Vapor Barrier Design and Conditions

A vapor barrier is any form of protection against uncontrolled migration of moisture into the data center. It could be simply a matter of plugging holes, or it could mean retrofitting the structure of the data center to encapsulate the room. The added expense involved in creating an effective vapor barrier will be returned in greater efficiencies in the environmental support equipment.

The following points should be considered to provide an effective vapor barrier:

- **Avoid unnecessary openings.** Open access windows, mail slots, etc., should not be a part of the data center design. These allow exposure to more loosely controlled surrounding areas.

- **Seal perimeter breaches.** All penetrations leading out into uncontrolled areas should be blocked and sealed. For more information, see "Supply Air Plenum Integrity" on page 121.

- **Seal doorways.** Doors and doorways should be sealed against unnecessary air and vapor leaks. Place high-efficiency gaskets and sweeps on all perimeter doors.

- **Paint perimeter walls.** Paint all perimeter walls from the structural deck to the structural ceiling to limit the migration of moisture through the building material surfaces.

- **Seal subfloor area.** Seal the subfloor to eliminate moisture penetration and surface degradation. The normal hardeners that are used in most construction will probably not be adequate to seal the subfloor. The procedure and additional materials for this process should be included in the building blueprints.

CHAPTER 9

Network Cabling Infrastructure

"From chaos comes order."

 - Friedrich Nietzsche

The network cabling infrastructure consists of all the devices and cabling that must be configured for the data center to be connected to its networks, as well as the cabling required to connect one device to another within a configuration (for example, connecting disk devices to servers).

This chapter contains the following sections:
- "Creating a Network Cabling Infrastructure"
- "Points of Distribution"
- "Avoiding Spaghetti"
- "Labeling and Color Coding"
- "Verification"

Creating a Network Cabling Infrastructure

Imagine that you have a bunch of data center devices and they need to be connected to each other. You could connect them using individual cables for every connection. Chapter 4, "Determining Data Center Capacities" described a set of racks, 40 Sun Fire 6800 servers with 4 Sun StorEdge racks connected to each Sun Fire server. The RLU definition for a Sun StorEdge rack contained 8 multi-mode fibre connections ($40 \times 4 \times 8$, or 1,280 multi-mode fibre cables). This makes 1,280 fibre cables running under the floor just to support disk connectivity to these configurations. Let's say you also want to manage the Sun StorEdge T3 arrays in these racks over your network. You need another 1,280 Cat5 cables to just the Sun StorEdge racks, plus 40 Cat5 cables to connect the Sun Fire 6800 servers to your administration network, plus 40 cables to connect the Sun Fire 6800 servers to only one of your production networks, plus 40 cables to connect the consoles of these devices. That's 2,680 separate cables running under the floor going to different devices in different locations on the floor. In an ideal world, each Sun Fire 6800 server and its 4 Sun StorEdge racks would be right next to each other. However, they probably aren't, so you have cables criss-crossing under the floor.

Now, suppose one of those cables goes bad and you need to replace it. If it's not labeled, you need to physically trace the cable under the floor. The probability is that the cable you need to trace is wrapped up in a bunch of other cables and will be difficult and time-consuming to trace, ensure that it is the correct cable, and replace. There is a better way to solve this problem. By knowing your connectivity requirements you can create a modular design using points of distribution (PODs) which minimize unnecessary cabling under the floor.

Determining Connectivity Requirements

Make sure you read Chapter 4, "Determining Data Center Capacities," and determine your connectivity requirements for each device.

The connectivity requirements will be based on the type of connections the device has (Cat5 or fibre) and how many of these connections you need for each device. For example, a Sun StorEdge T3 array has one fibre connection and two Cat5 connections, one for network connection and one for the physical console. You need the fibre connection to transfer data to and from the Sun StorEdge T3 array. To configure, administer, and monitor the Sun StorEdge T3 array through the network, you need a connection to the network port through its Cat5 interface. If you want access to the physical console as well, this is again through a Cat5 cable. Let's say you want network connectivity but not the physical console. For each Sun StorEdge T3 array you need one multi-mode fibre cable and one Cat5 cable. With eight Sun StorEdge T3 arrays in a rack, the connectivity requirement is eight multi-mode fibre and eight Cat5.

Modular Design

In the past, when the cabling requirements for machines were less (maybe one or two per machine), you could run the cables to one central point, usually the network room. However, as you can see from the previous example, the number of connections has increased by orders of magnitude. You can still run 2,680 cables back to the network room, but the data center design philosophy dictates that you keep the design as simple as possible.

Since we have segmented the floor into a given number of RLUs of particular types, we can define an area on the floor that contains a certain number of RLUs which will determine how many Cat5 and fibre connections the area will need. Repeat this process for all areas of the floor. Each of these clusters of RLUs, and more specifically, their network cabling requirements, can be looked at as a module. This also allows us to build in some fudge factor. It is as likely as not that, over time, some RLUs will be over their initial cabling requirements and others will be below. By grouping some of them together we have the flexibility (another part of the design philosophy) to allocate an extra connection from an RLU that is not in use to one that needs it. We can also locate support devices, switches, terminal servers, and Cat5 and fibre patch panels for this module somewhere within this cluster of RLUs.

You might need to connect a storage device on one side of the data center to a server on the opposite side. There are two ways to do this. You can use the logic contained in switches to move data from one device to another, or you can use the patch panels to cross-connect one patch panel port to another. This basic design allows you to keep connections local to an area for greater simplicity, but gives you the flexibility to connect (logically or physically) from one module to another.

Hierarchy of the Network Structure

The previously described design relies on the fundamental structure of logical networking that allows you to create a hierarchy of devices. The following figure shows an example hierarchy of devices.

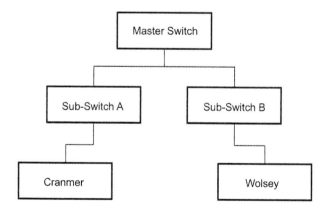

FIGURE 9-1 Hierarchy of Network Devices

Consider this example of a very simple network hierarchy structure. The machine Cranmer needs to send data to a machine called Wolsey. Cranmer sends the data to Sub-Switch A. Sub-Switch A does not have a direct connection to Wolsey so it sends out a request to ask if any device with a direct connection can send the data to Wolsey. The Master Switch responds, so Sub-Switch A sends the data to the Master

Switch. The Master Switch sends the data to Sub-Switch B which is directly connected to Wolsey and sends the data to Wolsey. This usually happens within a few hundredths of a millisecond. You could extend this hierarchy to thousands of machines and tens or hundreds of switches, 20 levels deep. The time required to get the data through will increase with the increased number of levels in the hierarchy (this is called latency), but the basic operation is the same.

Points of Distribution

A Point Of Distribution (POD) is a rack of devices and patches that manages a certain number of RLUs (which you can think of as a group of devices). PODs allow you to distribute both the physical and logical networking cables and networking equipment into modular and more manageable groups, and allow you to centralize any necessary cross-patching. All of the cabling from a group of devices can connect to the network through the POD. A data center might have dozens or hundreds of groups of devices, and each group can be managed by a POD. Network devices connect the PODs to the network room.

The use of this modular, hierarchical, POD design, and having a POD every 16 to 24 RLUs on the floor, allows you to have shorter cable runs from the machines and makes the cables easier to trace. It also avoids tangled cables ("spaghetti") under the floor.

Note – The components of a POD are contained in a rack of a given size, usually specified in terms of rack units (U). 1U is equal to 1.75 inches in height. A typical 7 foot rack contains about 6.5 feet of usable rack space, making it 45U tall (1.75" x 45 = 78.75"). When you calculate how many devices you can fit in your rack, you will need to know the number of Us of each device.

The POD rack contains three things:

- Network Terminal Servers (NTS)
- Cat5 and fibre ports for cross-patching
- Network sub-switches

Network Terminal Servers

A Network Terminal Server (NTS) is a device that allows you to connect the physical console of a device to a port. You can reach the NTS by way of the network, connect to that port, and then you are connected to the console of that device. Access to the console of a device is important for tasks such as installing the operating system, adding patches, or rebooting the machine. This can be done through the NTS.

It is not necessary for the device to be on the network to be connected to the NTS, but within a functioning data center, the devices probably will be on the network. Having the console on the network can be a potential security problem. However, there are ways to protect yourself. Most NTSs have an authentication system to help restrict access. Also, the NTSs would be on your administrative network, and one or more forms of authentication should be required to gain access to that network.

Network security is an important issue. For more information, go to `http://www.sun.com/blueprints/online.html` and type "network security" into the Search box.

Cross-Patch Ports

The Cat5 and fibre ports allow cross-patching when needed. These cross-patches are significantly fewer in number than if you were to run all the needed cables to a single central point. This increases ease of manageability and decreases cost.

The patches from each POD terminate in the network room. Also, each of the patches is uniquely identified with the same identifier (label) at both ends, in the POD and in the network room. They should also be tested to verify that they meet the specification you are using. There are devices, commonly called cable testers, that are attached to each end of the cable. Then a series of data streams are sent that verify that the cable meets its specification and the results compared against what the specifications should be. To meet specifications, the results must be within certain tolerances. Specifications for both Cat5 and multi-mode fibre are available from the IEEE.

Cable verification should be included in the contract with your network cabling supplier.

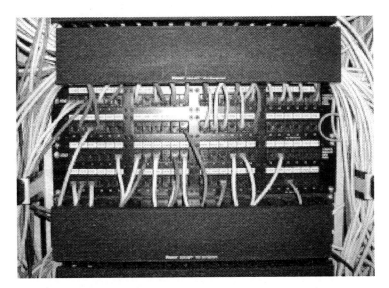

FIGURE 9-2 Cross-Patch Ports

The network equipment in a POD is more likely to change over time than the cross-patch ports. To design for this flexibility, the highest density patch panels should be used to minimize the space they take up in each POD. The highest density for Cat5 and fibre patch panels, as of this writing, is 48 ports of fibre in 5U and 48 ports of Cat5 in 2U. (See the note about Us on page 126.) If you need 48 ports of each, that's 96 cables! You need a way to keep all those cables organized. Cable management units for each of the two patch panels are 2U. The patch panel setup for a POD that contains 1 fibre patch panel, 1 Cat5 patch panel, and 2 cable management units is 11 U (19.25 in.). The wires that go from the patch panels in the PODs to the network room should be bundled together and run to the network room above the raised floor, usually in a separate cable tray in the ceiling plenum, to maximize air flow under the raised floor.

Sub-Switches

Let's say that you will have four networks in the data center. Three of these networks are for production and one is the administrative network. Each POD must have a sub-switch on the administrative network. You determine that you need connectivity to all production networks from each POD. So, for production and administrative network connectivity you need four sub-switches per POD. Each of these sub-switches is connected to a master switch for that network in the network room. Remember that you can only transfer data through the network hierarchy at the maximum rate of the narrowest device. If you have 100BaseT Ethernet feeding your servers on the production networks, and only a 100BaseT interface connecting that sub-switch to the master switch, one server could take up all the bandwidth to the master switch. In this case, it would be better to use a 1000BaseT interface to connect the sub-switches to their master switch.

Note – Since you have physical separation of logical networks in the POD based on each sub-switch, you could preconfigure all the ports on each sub-switch. This means when you need to connect a machine to the network, you just plug it in to the correct sub-switch. This allows for a minimum of human interaction with the configuration of the switch once it is in production. Remember, every time someone has to modify the configuration of a device, they inject the possibility of human error. By preconfiguring the switches, you considerably reduce this risk.

Cable Connectors

The RJ-45 connector is the de facto standard for Cat5 copper wiring. However, in fibre cabling you have several options: LC, SC, and ST type connectors. SC is currently the most common because it is the standard connector type for most current Gigabit Interface Converters (GBIC) used in fibre networking and SAN applications. The LC connector is half the size of an SC connector, and it is likely, since space is always at a premium, that LC will eventually surpass SC as the most common fibre connector type. In trying to design for future requirements, you should install fiber with LC connectors in your PODs. If you need to convert from LC to SC, you can use a device called a dongle. If necessary, you can use a similar type of dongle to convert the much older ST type connector to SC or LC.

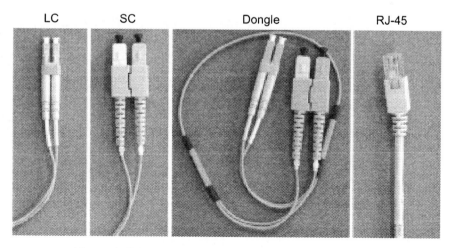

LC   SC   Dongle   RJ-45

FIGURE 9-3 Network Cable Connectors

Avoiding Spaghetti

Spaghetti is great on a plate with a nice Bolognese sauce. It isn't good in a data center. (See "Glossary" for a good Bolognese sauce recipe.) It is all too common for the network cabling in data centers to get tangled up on top of and under the floor due to bad or non-existent cabling schemes. Keep the following suggestions in mind:

- Use the correct length of Cat5 or fiber cables to go from point to point. This avoids the need to coil or otherwise bundle excess cable.

- Use cable ties to keep cables in ordered bundles.

- Route cables, whenever possible, under the tiles of the raised floors, preferably in cable trays. Don't lay cable on the ground where it can block air flow and create dust traps.

- Label each cable at both ends so that the floor doesn't need to be raised to follow cable routing. (See the following section, "Labeling and Color Coding.")

- Avoid messy cable routing on the floor as shown in the following figure. This creates several hazards and liability issues.

FIGURE 9-4 Spaghetti on the Floor

Labeling and Color Coding

There are labels on the patch panel ports, but you should label the cables as well, and *on both ends*. (Don't laugh. There are many data centers around the world at this very moment that have cables labeled only at one end.) If you label each end of each cable, most times you don't even have to open the floor. If a machine is having network connectivity problems, you can quickly determine which cable and port it is. If you won't be using patch panels, or you know that tracing cables could be problematic and time consuming, you might want to place labels every six feet along the length of each cable.

FIGURE 9-5 Labeling on a Patch Panel

These labels, just like labels for the patch panels, power outlets, and circuit breakers, need to be uniquely identified. Over the life of a data center you could go through a lot of cables. If you used a 2-character, 3-digit scheme (for example, AS257), you would have 675,324 usable, unique labels ($26 \times 26 \times 999 = 675,324$). That should be enough.

Color coding is also useful as an identifier. In the above scenario, you would need five colors: one for the administrative network, three for the production networks, and one for the NTSs. Using yellow cables, for example, for the administrative network implies a warning. These cables must be plugged only into the administrative network. This makes it easier to identify which sub-switch is on which network. You should have a label on the switch, but somebody might forget to check the label. It's much harder to miss plugging a purple cable into the sub-switch with all the purple cables. If you can't use different colored cables, consider using color coded labels on the cables.

Verification

Each patch panel port should be verified and certified by the installer as part of the contract. You should also have cable testers, both Cat5 and fibre, available in the data center. With these you can verify that the patch-panel ports were done correctly and, if you have questionable cables, you can find out whether they are good or not. This helps to eliminate doubt.

The ability to verify cables and ports is core to the design. That's why the quote *"...when you have excluded the impossible, whatever remains, however improbable, must be the truth"* is at the top of the "Data Center Design Criteria" chapter.

CHAPTER **10**

Shipping, Receiving, and Staging

"Inside outside outside inside"

- *Classix Nouveaux*

In the data center design, a shipping, receiving, and staging area is an important consideration, particularly if the equipment will involve many reconfigurations in the lifetime of the center. Often, shipping and receiving take place in one area, usually near a loading dock. Staging can happen in the same area, or it could be in a separate location (recommended). Finally, storage facilities must be considered.

This chapter has the following sections:

- "Loading Dock"
- "Staging Area"
- "Storage"

Loading Dock

The loading dock design and construction are part of the basic architecture of the building, and an adequate loading dock should be part of your site selection criteria. If your company has a separate Shipping and Receiving department, they will probably have the last word in determining how the loading dock is set up.

FIGURE 10-1 Loading Docks With a Large Area in Which Trucks Can Easily Maneuver

It is not within the scope of this book to look at all the possible configurations, but some important factors should be kept in mind during the planning stages:

- **Safety.** Safety should be the primary concern of loading dock design. Loading, unloading, warehousing, and distribution are rated among the most hazardous of industries. A single accident can cost thousands to millions of dollars in insurance, downtime, and liability costs. Consider safety systems carefully. Good lighting, good drainage, good ventilation, vehicle restraints, dock bumpers, striping, indicator lights, wheel chocks, safety barriers, and hydraulic dock levelers are just a few of these considerations.

- **Flexibility.** Advances occur in trucking and material handling which can dramatically effect the design of the docking facilities. Future trends must be taken into consideration. Loading docks must be equipped with features that ensure workability and safety throughout its lifetime.

- **Durability.** Loading docks take a lot of abuse. The effort and expense of using quality materials and durable designs will pay for itself in the long run.

- **Bigger trucks.** Trucks are getting longer and wider. Many trucks are now 102 inches wide and can be 80 feet long, or longer. If such large-capacity trucks will be used, the docking area and the maneuvering area must be designed to accommodate them.

- **Truck access.** Some truck trailer floors are as low as 36 inches to increase ceiling height. To accommodate these trucks, the dock must have portable ramps, truck levelers, dock levelers, or some other way to equalize the distance between dock floor and trailer floor.

- **Separation from data center.** Access points from the loading/shipping/receiving areas should not open directly into the data center due to the problems of contamination and the loss of air pressure.

- **Climate control.** Dock seals and shelters help to maintain the internal climate, protect merchandise, create security, save energy, and keep the area safe from rain, snow, and wind that pose a threat to human safety.

- **Use specialists.** Every loading dock has its own special requirements. Consult with qualified loading dock specialists during the design stages.

Shipping and Receiving

Shipping and receiving will usually occur at the loading dock. Computer equipment can be large, heavy, and have special requirements such as the use of air-ride equipped trucks, but many shipping and receiving groups don't consider these factors for their loading docks. Below is a brief checklist of things to consider.

These areas should have the following features:

- Protection from rain, snow, wind, etc.

- Accessible by large equipment, forklifts, pallet jacks, trucks, etc.

- Area for maneuverability of heavy equipment and vehicles. This must take the turning radius of large vehicles into consideration. Also consider ventilation areas for exhaust fumes.

- The path from receiving to the data center should be unobstructed, have wide enough access, and have ramps available at different levels.

- Secure access points.

- Air-ride equipped trucks for transporting equipment.

For information on ramps and lifts, see the section "Ramps and Lifts" on page 72 of Chapter 6, "Implementing a Raised Floor."

Staging Area

At least one dedicated staging area should be part of the data center design. Staging is an area between the loading dock and the equipment's final destination, and is often used for equipment configuration. Equipment coming from receiving on its way to the data center, as well as equipment moving from the data center out to storage or shipping, will usually be processed in the staging area.

This area should be outside the data center, but should be maintained within similar parameters. Contamination will be generated by packing, unpacking, and component handling and this must be isolated from the operational equipment. The staging area also involves a lot more human and machine traffic that can add to and stir up contaminants.

- Videotaping of the packing and unpacking process is good for having a record of how things fit into place.

- Equipment should go through a verification process (also known as "burn-in"). Verification test suites (VTS) are sometimes available from the company supplying the equipment. This process is usually separate from the burn-in done later after racks are placed in the data center and the operating system and software is loaded.

- The packing and unpacking of equipment can create a lot of contaminants, so this should always be done in the staging area.

- Equipment should be stored, if even for a short time, in the staging area. The same security measures that limit and monitor physical access should be used in the staging area just as they would be used in the data center itself.

Packing and Unpacking Area

One of the things often overlooked in a staging area is the space required to pack and unpack equipment. A Sun Fire 15000 server requires a minimum of 18 linear feet to unpack the machine from its shipping material. Just to pack or unpack this machine, you need a clear area 18 feet long by 10 feet wide (180 sq ft). It's better to have too much space than not enough, so consider allowing 20 feet by 10 feet (200 sq ft) for this process.

This area must also be able to handle the weight requirements of all the equipment. Consider the amount of packing and unpacking you might do in parallel. There is usually more than one rack for a single configuration in the data center, and these racks often arrive at the loading dock at the same time. Realistically, if you only have one area of 200 sq ft, you can only unpack one of these racks at a time.

Storage

It is often necessary to retain packing materials in case something must be shipped back to the vendor, for example, in the event of a component failure. Since this material can create contaminants, it should be stored in an area with no running computer equipment.

FIGURE 10-2 Outdoor Storage Sheds

Packing materials can also take up a lot of space, so using expensive raised floor space, or even office space, is probably not a cost-effective solution. You might also need to find economic storage for large quantities of inexpensive equipment, like network cable. On the other hand, expensive equipment and critical spare parts should be stored in the data center or staging area, because restricting access to this type of equipment is prudent.

Consider the following:

- Will the storage area be close to the data center? If not, how far away?
- Will storage be outsourced?
- Document how equipment was packed for ease in repacking. Label everything!
- How much space will be needed for storage materials?

CHAPTER 11

Avoiding Hazards

"The ice age is coming, the sun's zooming in, a meltdown expected, the wheat is growing thin, a nuclear error, but I have no fear."

   - The Clash

Potential hazards in a data center can range from mildly inconvenient to devastating. Some are difficult to avoid, but knowing what the potential hazards are in the data center area is the first step in preparing to avoid or combat them.

This chapter contains the following sections:

- "Types of Hazards"
- "Personnel Health and Safety"
- "Fire"
- "Flooding"
- "Earthquakes"
- "Miscellaneous Disasters"
- "Security Problems"
- "Noise Problems"

Types of Hazards

Hazards for the data center can run the gamut from natural disasters to human-created accidents. Weather and seismic activity constitute some of the potential problems, and knowing the local histories of these phenomena is essential to protecting the data center, and people, against them.

Some natural hazards are:

- Fire from electrical storms
- Flooding from rain, overflows, runoff
- Earthquakes
- High winds
- Hurricanes
- Tornados

Some human-created hazards are:

- Fire from electrical short circuits
- Flooding from equipment failure, leaking plumbing, sprinkler systems
- Vibration caused by construction, large equipment, nearby industry
- Noise from data center computers, large machinery, nearby industry

Personnel Health and Safety

From the very earliest design phases of the data center, the most important concern in disaster avoidance and recovery is for human health and safety. Equipment is important, but it always comes second to people.

Manual controls for various data center support systems should be conveniently located. Controls for fire, HVAC, power, abort or silence, and an independent phone line should be grouped by appropriate doorways. All controls should be clearly labeled, and concise operating instructions should be available at each station.

Keep the following human safety guidelines in mind when planning the data center.

- Keep room personnel to the absolute minimum
- Authorized personnel should be trained to respond to emergency situations
- Monitor air quality in the room
- Ensure that personnel are able to exit the room or building efficiently
- Avoid blockages and doors that won't open easily from the inside
- Avoid long rows of racks or equipment with no breaks

- Clearly mark fire extinguishers and position them at regular intervals in the room
- Clearly mark first aid kits and position them at regular intervals in the room

---

Fire

Fire can occur in a data center by either mechanical failure, intentional arson, or by natural causes, though the most common sources of fires are from electrical systems or hardware. Whether fire is measured in its threat to human life, damage to equipment, or loss of business due to disruption of services, the costs of a fire can be staggering. The replacement cost for the devastation caused by a fire can number in the tens or hundreds of millions of dollars.

A fire can create catastrophic effects on the operations of the room. A large-scale fire can damage electronic equipment and the building structure beyond repair. Contamination from smoke and cinder from a smoldering fire can also damage hardware and incur heavy costs in cosmetic repairs. Even if the actual fire is avoided, discharge of the fire suppression medium could possibly damage hardware.

Fire Prevention

Several steps should be taken to avoid fires. Compliance with NFPA 75 will greatly increase the fire safety in the center. The following precautions should be taken in the design and maintenance of the data center and support areas:

- **No smoking.** Smoking should never be allowed in the data center. Signs should be posted at entryways and inside. If you think this could be a problem, designing in a nearby smoking area for breaks will reduce or eliminate smoking in the data center.

- **No combustible materials.** Keep flammable chemicals and combustible materials out of the data center. Store packing materials in a separate staging or storage area.

- **Check HVAC reheat coils.** Check the reheat coils on the air conditioner units periodically. If left unused for a while, they can collect dust that will smolder and ignite when they are heated up.

- **Check suppression system.** Sprinkler systems and/or FM200 fire suppression systems should be periodically checked. Also, they should be of a type triggered by heat, not smoke.

- **Preserve the data center "cocoon."** Periodically inspect the data center perimeter for breaches into more loosely controlled areas. Block any penetrations. An alarm or suppression system discharge caused by conditions outside the center is unacceptable.

- **Have a disaster response plan.** To maximize human safety and minimize fire damage, create a detailed disaster response plan. All data center personnel should be properly trained in the procedures, and the plan should be periodically reviewed. In an emergency, you might not be able to get into the building, so it is a good idea to keep a copy of the plan, along with a company phone list with home numbers, at the homes of several employees.

- **Easy access to fire extinguishers.** All personnel should know where extinguishers are and how to operate them.

Physical Barriers

The first line of fire defense and containment is the actual building structure. The rooms of the data center (and storage rooms) must be isolated by fire-resistant walls that extend from the concrete subfloor deck to the structural ceiling. The floor and ceiling must also be constructed of noncombustible or limited combustible materials able to resist the fire for at least an hour. Appropriately controlled firebreaks must also be present.

The HVAC system should be dedicated to the controlled area of the data center. If this is not possible, appropriately rated fire dampers must be placed in all common ducts or plenums.

Fire Detection Systems

When data center fires occur, they are commonly due to the electrical system or hardware components. Short circuits can generate heat, melt components, and start a fire. Computer room fires are often small and smoldering with little effect on the room temperatures.

The early warning fire detection system should have the following features:

- It should be a heat detection type.

- It should be installed and maintained in accordance with NFPA 72E, *Standard on Automatic Fire Detectors*.

- Each installation should be engineered for the specific area it will protect, allowing for air current patterns.

- Depending on local code, an automatic detection system might need to be installed under the raised floor, since electrical outlets are there.

- Since it can get very noisy in the data center, a visual alert, usually a red flashing siren light, should also be included in the system.

Fire Suppression Systems

A passive suppression system reacts to detected fire hazards with no manual intervention. The most common forms of passive suppression systems are sprinkler systems or chemical suppression systems.

Modern gas systems are friendlier to hardware and, if the fire is stopped before it can do any serious damage, the data center might be able to continue operations. Water sprinklers are sometimes a viable alternative if saving the building is more important than saving the equipment (a water system will probably cause irreparable damage to the hardware). Gas systems are effective, but are also shorter lived. Once the gas is discharged, there is no second chance, whereas a water system can continue until the fire is out. Water systems are highly recommended in areas that contain a lot of combustible materials such as storerooms.

These decisions must be weighed, but in the end it could be local ordinance, the insurance company, or the building owner who will determine what suppression system must be installed. There is no reason why multiple systems can't be used, if budget allows.

Following are descriptions of a few different suppression systems. Note that the last two are *not* recommended, but are described in the event that such legacy systems exist in the facility. If either or both of these are in place, they should be changed out for safer systems.

- **FM200.** This is the recommended suppression system. The FM200 uses the gas heptafluoropropane which is quickly dispersed around the equipment. It works by literally removing heat energy from the fire to the extent that the combustion reaction cannot be sustained. It works quickly, is safe for people, doesn't damage hardware, won't interrupt electrical circuits, and requires no post-discharge cleanup. With this system there is the possibility that the data center will be back in business almost immediately after a fire.

- **Dry pipe sprinkler.** Dry pipe sprinkler systems are similar to wet pipe systems with the exception that the pipes are not flooded with water until detection of a fire threat. The advantage is less likelihood of leaks. The disadvantages are the longer amount of time before discharge and the possibility of ruining equipment. If this system is used, a mechanism should be installed that will deactivate all power, including power from UPSs and generators, before the system activates.

- **Wet pipe sprinkler.** Wet pipe sprinkler systems use pipes that are full at all times, allowing the system to discharge immediately upon the detection of a fire threat. The advantage is speed in addressing the fire. The disadvantages are the possibility of leaks and of ruining equipment. If this system is used, a mechanism should be installed that will deactivate all power, including power from UPSs and generators, before the system activates.

- **Halon 1301.** *Not recommended.* Halon is an ozone-depleting gas that has been replaced in favor of the more environmentally friendly FM200. Halon 1301 systems are no longer in production as of January 1994, and legacy systems can only be recharged with existing supplies.

- **Carbon dioxide.** *Not recommended.* Carbon dioxide is a very effective fire suppressant but is not safe for people. At the minimum design concentration as a total flooding fire suppressant (34 percent), carbon dioxide is lethal. At lower concentrations it can cause severe health problems.

Manual Fire Suppression

Manual means of fire suppression should also be on hand in the event that automatic systems fail. Following are descriptions of the two backup systems:

- **Portable fire extinguishers.** Portable extinguishers should be placed at strategic stations throughout the room. These should be unobstructed and clearly marked. Signs indicating the location of the extinguisher stations should be placed high enough to be seen over tall cabinets and racks from across the room. Tile lifters should also be located at each extinguisher station to allow access to the subfloor void, both for inspection and for addressing a fire.

- **Manual pull stations.** Manual pull stations should be installed at strategic points in the room. In areas where gas suppression systems are used, there should be a means of manual abort. In designs where it is necessary to hold the abort button to maintain the delay in discharge, it is essential that a means of communication be available within reach.

FIGURE 11-1 Fire Extinguisher With a Highly Visible Sign

Flooding

Like fire, flooding can be caused by either equipment failure or by natural causes. Consider the following:

- How often, if ever, does flooding occur around the data center area?
- Can the data center be located in a higher area, safe from flooding?
- Will you need moisture sensors and fast-acting pumps?

Avoiding Leaks

While the design should attempt to prohibit water pipes from passing through the data center, sometimes this cannot be avoided. If you are forced into this situation, some or all of the precautions below should be considered.

- Troughs to channel water out of the data center should be installed underneath pipes. These troughs should have the same or greater flow rate as the pipes themselves.

- It is possible to have a pipe within a pipe. If the interior pipe develops a leak, the water would be contained in the outer pipe.

- Water detection sensors should be placed along the runs of the pipes and at plumbing joints where most leaks are likely to start.
- In cold climates and near HVAC units, insulate the pipe to prevent freezing.

Earthquakes

Some parts of the world have little or no history of earth tremors while others are plagued by them. For those building in Iowa, you probably aren't too concerned about earthquakes, whereas those building in California or Tokyo should consider the following:

- How often, if ever, do earthquakes occur in the region?
- Is the data center site built to withstand seismic disturbances?
- Can the data center be located on lower floors where there would be less sway?
- Should equipment be held down with seismic restraints?
- Can racks be secured to the floor and ceiling as a means of seismic restraint?
- Other steps required to ensure the safety of personnel should be outlined in local building codes.

Miscellaneous Disasters

There are many possible disasters to consider, and the effects of most will fall into categories that cause one or more problems.

- **Wind-based (hurricanes and tornados).** Use the same appropriate guidelines for earthquakes, as these events will cause the building to shake or vibrate.
- **Water-based (severe storms and tsunamis).** Use the appropriate guidelines for water penetration and leak detection on doors and windows.
- **Electrical-based (lightning and thunderstorms).** Use adequate grounding for devices and a very good signal reference grid. Also use lightning rods on the exterior of the building that go to a separate earth ground, so impedance does not build up in the standard grounding system.

Security Problems

The security of the data center is critical. Data centers not only contain valuable computer hardware, but the data in the machines is usually worth exponentially more than the 10s or 100s of millions of dollars that the equipment costs.

Access should be restricted to only authorized and trained personnel. Several levels of barriers should be in place. The use of "traps" (a space between two doors) is a good idea for security as well as preventing the infiltration of particulate matter. People enter the exterior door and the interior door cannot be opened until the exterior door is closed. The data center should be positioned so that it does not use an exterior wall. Avoid exterior windows in your data center. If your data center does use an exterior wall, place barriers on the outside of the wall to slow down vehicles that might try to smash through. (This might sound ridiculous, but it has happened.)

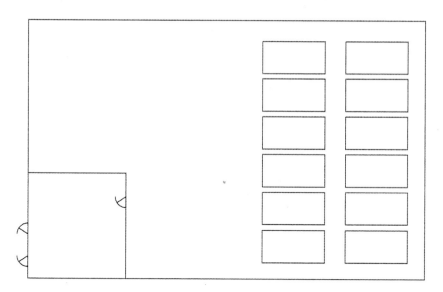

FIGURE 11-2 Trap Between the Data Center and Outside Area

For many corporations, their information is their business. If it sounds like you are fortifying this thing to be a mini Fort Knox, you are on the right path. Consider the following:

- What level of security will the area need?
- What is the current security of the area?
- Are there windows or doors that could prove to be a security risk? Can they be blocked?

- Where will the Command Center be located? Will it have a separate entrance?
- Will the data center only be accessible through the Command Center?
- Will people be able to remotely access the data center from anywhere? Will there be access restrictions to certain portions?
- What portions of the data center will be remotely accessible?
- Is a surveillance system (video cameras) an option?

Noise Problems

With processors getting faster and disks getting more dense, the cooling requirements in data centers are rising. This means more fans and blowers to move more conditioned air. Noise can be a big problem in some data centers. The use of Command Centers, and devices like network terminal servers that allow remote access to a machine, allow users to work in a less noisy environment. However, you will need to have people in your data center some of the time.

Ear protection should be used in particularly noisy rooms, and might even be required. The installation of noise cancelling equipment is useful but expensive. If people are working remotely most of the time, it might not be worth the cost. Ear protection might be adequate. If you do have people in the data center quite often, the investment in noise cancellation equipment might be worthwhile.

CHAPTER **12**

Environmental Contaminants

"The kitchen floor is in the most disgustingly filthy state that it is possible for the human brain to conceive. Amateur microbiologists amongst you will find much down there that will enthrall and fascinate. Very likely species, as yet unknown to science, are breeding freely underfoot even as I speak. It is possible I am kneeling, all unbeknownst, on a cure for the common cold, herpes, and male pattern baldness all rolled into one. But, rule such considerations out of your minds and CLEAN THIS FRIGGING FLOOR!!!"

   - Lenny Henry as Gareth Blackstock in "Chef!"

Particles, gasses, and other contaminants can impact the sustained operations of the computer hardware in a data center. These contaminants can take many forms, some foreseeable and some not. The list of possible contaminants could be localized to the district (local factory pollutants, airborne dusts, etc.), or they could be generated more locally somewhere at the site. Airborne dust, gasses, and vapors should be kept within defined limits to minimize their impact on people and hardware.

This chapter contains the following sections:

- "Contaminant Types and Sources"
- "Effects of Contaminants"
- "Avoiding Contamination"

Contaminant Types and Sources

There are two criteria for a substance to be considered a contaminant in relation to a data center environment:

- It must be potentially damaging to hardware or people.
- It must be able to migrate to areas where it can cause damage.

Contaminants that affect people and equipment are typically airborne, so, obviously, it is important to limit the amount of potential contaminants that cycle through the data center air supply to prolong the life of all electronic devices. Potential contaminants can also be settled, making them harder to measure. Care must be taken that these aren't agitated by people or mechanical processes.

Measures should be taken to prevent air contaminants such as metal particles, atmospheric dust, solvent vapors, corrosive gasses, soot, airborne fibers, or salts from entering, or being generated within, the data center. Airborne particulate levels should be maintained within the limits of Federal Standard 209e, *Airborne Particulate Cleanliness Classes in Cleanrooms and Clean Zones, Class 100,000*. This standard defines air quality classes for clean zones based on airborne particulate considerations. Class 100,000 is generally accepted as appropriate for data center environments. In the absence of hardware exposure limits, applicable human exposure limits from OSHA, NIOSH, or the ACGIH should be used. ASHRAE Standard 62 is an adequate guideline for both operator safety and hardware exposure. See Appendix B, "Bibliography and References," for more information regarding these agencies and organizations.

Gaseous Contaminants

Excessive concentrations of certain gasses can cause corrosion and failure in electronic components. Gasses are of particular concern because of the recirculating airflow pattern of the data center. The data center's isolation from outside influences can multiply the detrimental influences of any gasses in the air, because they are continually cycled through equipment for repeated attack.

Gasses particularly disruptive to electronic components include chlorine compounds, ammonia and its derivatives, oxides of sulfur and petrol hydrocarbons. TABLE 12-1 outlines limits for various gasses that could pose a threat to hardware. These should be used as guidelines and not as absolute limits. Numerous other factors, such as the moisture content of the air, can influence environmental corrosivity and gaseous contaminant transfer at lower levels. Higher concentrations of these levels should be a concern.

TABLE 12-1 Recommended Gas Limits

Chemical Name	Formula	ASHRAE	OSHA (PEL)	ACGIH	NIOSH
Acetic Acid	CH_3COOH	Not defined	10 ppm	Not defined	Not defined
Ammonia	NH	3500 mg/m^3	350 ppm	25 ppm	Not defined
Chlorine	C1	2100 mg/m^3	31 ppm (c)	Not defined	0.5 ppm (c)
Hydrogen Chloride	HC1	Not defined	5 ppm (c)	Not defined	Not defined
Hydrogen Sulfide	H_2S	50 mg/m^3	320 ppm (c)	10 ppm	10 ppm
Ozone	O_3	235 mg/m^3	30.1 ppm	Not defined	Not defined
Petrol-hydrocarbons	C_nH_n	Not defined	500 ppm	75 ppm	300 ppm
Sulfur Dioxide	SO2	80 mg/m^3	35 ppm	2 ppm	0.5 ppm (c)
Sulfuric Acid	H2SO4	Not defined	1 ppm	Not defined	1 ppm (c)

PEL = Permissible Exposure Limit
ppm = Parts Per Million
mg/m^3 = Micrograms Per Cubic Meter
(c) = Ceiling

Note – In the absence of appropriate hardware exposure limits, health exposure limits should be used.

Gasses From Outside

Many chemicals used in normal office cleaning can damage sensitive computer equipment. Out-gassing from these products or direct contact with hardware components can cause failure. Certain biocide treatments used in building air handlers are also inappropriate for data centers, because they are not formulated for the airstream of a recirculating air system.

Gaseous influences can also come from:

- Ammonia and phosphates from agricultural processes
- Chemicals from manufacturing processes
- Exhaust from nearby roads and freeways
- Moisture from sea mists

Particulate Contaminants

The most harmful contaminants are often overlooked because they are so small. Most particles smaller than 10 microns are not usually visible to the naked eye, and these are the ones most likely to migrate into areas where they can do damage. Particulates as big as 1,000 microns can become airborne, but their active life is short and they are typically arrested by most filtration systems. Submicronic particles are more dangerous to the data center environment because they remain airborne much longer and can bypass filters. Some of the most harmful dust particle sizes are 0.3 microns and smaller. These often exist in large quantities, and can easily clog the internal filters of components. They have the ability to agglomerate into large masses, and to absorb corrosive agents under certain psychrometric conditions. This poses a threat to moving parts and sensitive contacts. It also creates the possibility of component corrosion.

Measuring airborne particulate concentration in the data center is useful in determining air quality. Your HVAC contractor can probably help with this, or recommend an air quality engineer.

The removal of airborne particulate matter should be done with a filtering system, and the filters should be replaced as part of the regular maintenance of the data center. See "Filtration" on page 159 for more information.

Human Movement

Human movement within the data center space is probably the single greatest source of contamination. Normal movement can dislodge tissue fragments, dander, hair, or fabric fibers from clothing. The opening and closing of drawers or hardware panels, or any metal-to-metal activity, can produce metal filings. Simply walking across the floor can agitate settled contaminants.

All unnecessary activity and processes should be avoided in the data center, and access should be limited only to trained personnel. All personnel working in the room, including temporary employees and janitorial staff, should be trained in the basic sensitivities of the hardware and to avoid unnecessary contact. Tours of the facility are sometimes necessary, but these should be limited and traffic should be restricted to avoid accidental contact with equipment.

The best solution to keeping human activity to a minimum in the data center is to design in a Command Center with a view into the data center room. Almost all operations of the center will take place here, and those visiting the facilities can see the equipment from there. The data center should never be situated in such a way that people must go through the equipment room to get to unrelated parts of the building.

Subfloor Work

Hardware installation and reconfiguration involves a lot of subfloor activity, and settled contaminants can be disturbed, forcing them up into the equipment cooling airstreams. This is a particular problem if the subfloor deck has settled contaminants or has not been sealed. Unsealed concrete sheds fine dust particles and is also susceptible to efflorescence (mineral salts brought to the surface of the deck through evaporation or hydrostatic pressure). It is important to properly seal the subfloor deck and to clean out settled contaminants on a regular basis.

Stored Items

The storage and handling of hardware, supplies, and packing materials can be a major source of contamination. Cardboard boxes and wooden skids or palettes lose fibers when moved and handled. Particles of these have been found in the examination of sample subfloor deposits. The moving and handling of stored items also agitates settled contaminants already in the room. Also, many of these materials are flammable and pose a fire hazard. All of these are good arguments for making a staging area for packing and unpacking an important design criteria.

FIGURE 12-1 and FIGURE 12-2 show unnecessary clutter and particulate matter in a data center room.

FIGURE 12-1 Unnecessary Items Stored in the Data Center

FIGURE 12-2 Particulate Matter and Junk on the Floor

Particulate From Outside

Air introduced into the data center can be a source of contamination, especially if the filtering system is inadequate. It is important to know what dust and airborne chemicals could possibly come in from the outside environment. In particular, consider local agricultural activities, quarries, or masonry fabrication facilities. With this knowledge, plan the data center filtering system to arrest these particulates.

Effects of Contaminants

Destructive interactions between airborne particulate and electronic equipment can happen in many ways, some of which are outlined in the following subsections.

Physical Interference

Hard particles with a tensile strength at least 10 percent greater than the component material can remove material from the component surface by abrasive action or embedding. Soft particles might not damage the component surface, but can agglomerate (stick together) as the result of electrostatic charge build-up and cause clogging. If these particles are tacky, they can collect with other particulate matter.

Corrosive Failure

Component failures can occur from the corrosion of electrical contacts caused by certain types of particulate. Some particulates absorb water vapor and gaseous contaminants which adversely affect electrical components. Salts can grow in size by absorbing water vapor (nucleating). If the area is sufficiently moist, salts can grow large enough to physically interfere with a mechanism, or cause damage by forming corrosive salt solutions.

Short Circuits

The accumulation of certain types of particles on circuit boards and other components can create conductive pathways, thus creating short circuits. Many types of particulate are not inherently conductive, but can become conductive by absorbing moisture from the air. When this happens, the problems can range from intermittent malfunctions to component failures. To avoid this problem, care should be taken with both the proper filtration of air and careful control of humdification.

Thermal Failure

Thermal failures occur when cooling air cannot reach the components. Clogging of filtered devices can cause restricted airflow resulting in overheating of components. Heavy layers of accumulated dust on hardware components can form an insulative layer that can lead to heat-related failures. Regular replacement of air filters and cleaning of components will help to avoid this problem.

In one data center, plastic sheeting designed to contain particulate from a decommissioned server was actually causing thermal outages in an online server three feet away. The fans sucked the plastic just close enough to block inlets and overheat the system. Engineers couldn't find the problem because, when the system shut down, the fans stopped and the plastic dropped away. Plastic sheeting should be taped down to avoid this problem.

Avoiding Contamination

All surfaces within the controlled zone of the data center should be kept clean. This should be done by:

- **Keeping contaminants out.** Keeping contaminants from entering the data center should be done by minimizinging traffic through the room, adequate air filtering, avoidance of improper chemical use, and positive pressurization of the room. Also, a properly constructed data center uses only non-shedding and non-gassing materials. If the data center is a retrofit of an existing structure, it might be necessary to change out or seal some existing construction materials.

- **Regularly scheduled cleanings.** Cleanings should be performed by trained professionals on a regular basis. These cleanings should be done with the same concern and regularity as data backups.

Unfortunately, the data center cannot be a hermetically sealed environment. It must have several breaches for both humans and atmosphere. These are points of potential exposure to contaminants and must be clearly addressed in the design of the center.

Exposure Points

Breaches in the controlled zone of the data center must be controlled and monitored. All doors must fit snugly in their frames and be sealed with gaskets and sweeps. Automatic doors should be carefully controlled to avoid accidental triggering, especially by people without proper security clearance. A remote door trigger might be necessary so that personnel pushing carts can easily open the doors. In highly sensitive areas, a design with double sets of doors and a buffer in between will limit direct exposure to outside contamination.

To maintain environmental control, the data center is an isolated cocoon. Windows leading to uncontrolled parts of the building should be avoided. Also, seal all penetrations between the data center and adjacent areas. Do not share subfloor or ceiling plenums with any other part of the building. The subfloor void is of particular concern and is covered in the following subsection.

FIGURE 12-3 Unfilled Void Between Data Center Room and Subfloor Plenum

Damaged or poorly protected building materials are often sources of contamination. Unprotected concrete, masonry block, plaster, or gypsum wall-board will deteriorate over time, shedding fine particulate into the airstream. Corrosion on parts of the air conditioning system past the filters can also release particulate.

Subfloor Void

The subfloor void in a downward-flow air conditioning system functions as the supply air plenum. This area is pressurized by forced conditioned air, which is then introduced to the data center room through perforated tiles. Since all air moving into the room must travel through the subfloor void, it is critical that this area be kept at a high level of cleanliness. Contaminant sources can include degrading building materials, operator activity, or infiltration from areas outside the controlled zone.

Clutter in the subfloor plenum should be avoided. Tangled cables or stored materials can form "air dams" that allow particulate matter to settle and accumulate. When these items are moved, the particulate is stirred up and reintroduced to the supply airstream. Store supplies in outside storage areas, and keep all subfloor cabling organized in wire basket cable trays.

All surfaces of the subfloor area, particularly the concrete deck and the perimeter walls, should be properly sealed, ideally before the raised floor is installed. Unsealed concrete, masonry, and similar materials degrade over time. Sealants and hardeners used in normal construction are not meant for the surfaces of a supply air plenum. Only appropriate materials and methodologies should be used in the encapsulation process. Here are some guidelines:

- Spray applications should never be used in an online data center. The spraying process forces sealant particulate into the supply airstream. Spray applications could be appropriate if used in the early stages of construction.

- Use a pigmented encapsulant. The pigmentation makes the encapsulant visible, ensuring thorough coverage and helping to indicate areas damaged over time.

- The encapsulant must have a high flexibility and low porosity to effectively cover the irregular surface textures and to minimize moisture migration and water damage.

- The encapsulant must not out-gas harmful contaminants, particularly in an online data center. Some encapsulants are highly ammoniated or contain other chemicals harmful to hardware. The out-gassing might not cause immediate failure but could contribute to corrosion of contacts, heads, or other components. If out-gassing is short lived and the area is well ventilated, this might not be a problem in a new construction data center.

Positive Pressurization and Ventilation

Positive pressurization of the data center applies outward air forces to doorways and other access points within the room, keeping outside air, insects, and particulate matter from entering. In a closed-loop, recirculating air conditioning system, very little outside air needs to be introduced, however, some outside air is required to maintain positive pressurization and ventilation. This air must also be filtered and conditioned. Ventilation is important to the health of the occasional operators and visitors in the data center, but the air required for positive pressurization will likely exceed what is needed for occupants. The introduction of outside air should be kept to the minimum necessary to achieve the positive pressurization and ventilation requirements of the room.

Normally, outside air quantities of about 5 percent new (make-up) air should be sufficient (ASHREA Handbook: Applications, Chapter 17). A volume of 15 CFM (Cubic Feet per Minute) outside air per occupant or workstation should be enough for the ventilation needs of the room (Uniform Building Code, Chapter 12).

In data centers with multiple rooms, the most sensitive areas should be the most highly pressurized.

Filtration

Warm air from the data center hardware returns to the HVAC units where it is cooled and reintroduced to the room to continue the cooling cycle. The air change rate in a data center is much greater than a typical office environment and proper filtration is essential to arresting airborne particulate. Without high efficiency filtration, particulate matter will be drawn into computers with the probability of clogging airflow, gumming up components, causing shorts, blocking the function of moving parts, and causing components to overheat.

The following figure shows the filters placed in the top of an HVAC unit.

FIGURE 12-4 HVAC Filters

The filters installed in recirculating air conditioners should have a minimum efficiency of 40 percent Atmospheric Dust-Spot Efficiency (ASHRAE Standard 52.1). Air from outside the building should be filtered with High Efficiency Particulate Air (HEPA) filters rated at 99.97 percent efficiency (DOP Efficiency MIL-STD-282) or greater. To prolong their life, the expensive high-efficiency filters should be protected by multiple layers of lower grade prefilters that are changed more frequently. The first line of defense should be low-grade 20 percent ASHRAE Atmospheric Dust-Spot Efficiency filters. The next level of filtration should consist of pleated or bag type filters with efficiencies between 60 and 80 percent. All of these filters should fit properly in the air handlers. Gaps around the filter panels decrease the filter efficiency. These gaps should be filled with appropriate materials such as stainless steel panels or custom filter assemblies.

Refer to the following table for a comparison of filter efficiencies. As the table demonstrates, low efficiency filters are almost totally ineffective at removing submicronic particulate from the air.

TABLE 12-2 Typical Efficiencies of Various Filters

ASHRAE 52-76 % of Dust-Spot Efficiency	% of Fractional Efficiencies		
	3.0 micron	1.0 micron	0.3 micron
25 to 30%	80%	20%	<5%
60 to 65%	93%	50%	20%
80 to 85%	99%	90%	50%
95%	>99%	92%	60%
DOP 95%	--	>99%	95%

Copyright 1995, American Society of Heating, Refrigerating and Air-Conditioning Engineers, Inc., www.ashrae.org. Reprinted by permission from ASHRAE Journal-June 1995.

Taking Out the Trash

Trash should never be allowed to collect in any part of the data center, even in designated trash receptacles. If there are trash receptacles, they should be removed from the center and emptied often. Loose papers, rags, and chemical containers all pose fire hazards.

Regularly Scheduled Cleanings

Hardware performance and longevity are important reasons to perform regularly scheduled cleanings of the data center. Contaminants, even in small quantities, infiltrate the room and settle on room surfaces and within machinery. Excessive exposure to contaminants will result in increased component failure and interruption of services. Even a well-designed and constructed data center will require regularly scheduled maintenance and cleanings. Data centers with design flaws or rough retrofits will require more extensive effort to maintain appropriate levels of cleanliness.

Another, possibly less obvious reason for maintaining a clean data center has to do with psychology. Operators working in a clean and organized data center will be more inclined to respect the room and keep it clean and organized, thus maintaining its efficiency. Visitors to the data center will show similar respect and interpret the overall appearance of the room as a commitment to quality and excellence.

When designing the data center, keep regularly scheduled decontaminations in mind. A well-designed data center is easy to maintain.

CHAPTER 13

Codes and Construction

"Is the Minister aware that planning procedures make building a bungalow in the 20th century slower than building a cathedral in the 12th century?"

   - Nigel Hawthorne as Sir Humphrey in "Yes, Minister"

To fully consider and implement the design of the data center, you have to construct a facility that will meet the project scope and also meet code. This chapter will try to keep you from drowning in the quagmire of code. It also covers a few construction details worth keeping in mind.

This chapter has the following sections:

■ "Codes"
■ "Construction Criteria"
■ "Pre-Hardware Installation Checklist"

Codes

Codes for construction of buildings are there for a good reason. As stated in many building codes, the purpose is to provide minimum standards to safeguard life and limb, health, property, and public welfare. This can be best accomplished by regulating and controlling the design, construction, quality of materials, use and occupancy, location, and maintenance of all buildings, structures, and certain equipment within the jurisdiction. From building a garage in Malibu, California, to building the Sears Tower in Chicago, codes prevent people from taking shortcuts, using inferior materials, ignoring basic human safety, and knowingly or unknowingly creating an unsafe structure. If there were no codes, buildings would catch fire and fall down a lot more often.

Who do we have to thank for building codes? Hammarabi, the Babylonian emperor, developed the first building code more than four thousand years ago. It was not the quagmire of codes in use today, but it stated in simple terms that if a building fell down and killed the owner, the builder would be put to death. Apparently it was up to the builder to decide what materials should be used to make a safe house for his client. Since his life was at stake, some real thought went into the structural design. The concern for building for the safety of the human occupants, at least, has continued and has developed into the complex swamp of codes used today.

However, there still is no universal code or set of codes that builders can follow throughout the world. There are, in fact, any number of codes, combinations of codes, and variations of codes, international, national, and local.

You have just stepped into the quagmire.

The Quagmire of Codes

There are several building code organizations within the United States that have created their own set of codes. For example, there is Building Officials and Code Administrators International, Inc. (BOCA), International Conference of Building Officials (ICBO), and Southern Building Code Congress International, Inc. (SBCCI). For fire codes, there is the International Fire Code (IFC), which is coordinated with the International Building Code (IBC). However, there is also the National Fire Protection Association (NFPA) who develop and publish *NFPA 75 Standard for the Protection of Electronic Computer/Data Processing Equipment* and *NFPA 1 Fire Prevention Code 2000.*

There are other codes that must be considered when designing a data center. Below is a listing of the types of codes, though this does not represent all possible codes.

- Building codes
- Plumbing codes
- Mechanical codes
- Electrical codes
- Fire codes
- Fire sprinkler ordinances
- Energy conservation codes
- Sewage codes

All of the codes listed could be considered building codes in that they relate to the construction or remodeling of a site. Many of these codes are interdependent, and one code might refer to another code. One code might mention that you must have a 1-hour fire rated wall, but that the specifications for this are in another code. Your local code authority might say "Yes, the specs are in *that* code but you should use the specs in *this* code instead." The two codes that give these specifications might or might not be the same. Another possibility is that you would need to use more than one code to determine what your local inspector will agree is a 1-hour fire rated wall.

Also, some codes are identical, but masquerade under different names. For example, NFPA 70 is the same as the National Electrical Code.

The International Fire Code is yet another part of the quagmire. It is coordinated with the International Building Code. But it is maintained by a separate organization, the International Fire Code Institute. The IBC is published by BOCA. Even though BOCA publishes the IBC, they also publish state-specific building codes for Kentucky, Michigan, Ohio, and Virginia. Why it is called the International Building Code when even separate states in the U.S., not to mention other countries, might use a different building code? That's hard to answer. Just because something says it is international doesn't make it so.

There is also the NFPA that develops and publishes *NFPA 75 Standard for the Protection of Electronic Computer/Data Processing Equipment* as well as the *NFPA 1 Fire Prevention Code 2000*. They publish *NFPA 70* which, while widely adopted in the U.S. and elsewhere in the world, is like any of the above code: subject to interpretation.

So, the problem facing the data center designer is: Which building codes must you adhere to? You should be concerned with the codes used in the jurisdiction in which the data center will be constructed, keeping in mind that these codes are subject to the interpretation of the building authorities in the jurisdiction where the data center will be built.

A case in point: A company decided to put power distribution units (PDUs) beneath the raised floor in data centers in San Diego, California, and Austin, Texas. No problem! The local code was interpreted in such a way that putting PDUs beneath the raised floor tiles was within code. The same company also considered putting PDUs under the raised floor in their facility in Hillsboro, Oregon. However, the electrical engineering firm and the project management firm, knowledgeable about the way things work in Hillsboro, said they didn't think the code authorities in the area would approve the use of PDUs under a raised floor. The electrical engineering firm and the project management firm met with the building officials in the area and proposed a good case for using PDUs under raised floor. However, code officials maintained that the use of PDUs under the floor would not get code approval. In the way these officials interpreted the code, PDUs under the raised floor would not pass code. It is also important to note that these discussions occurred before construction of the data center started, during the design phase. This forward thinking was also a money saver, because these determinations were made before PDUs had been ordered.

Whatever codes have been adopted for your local jurisdiction, they are all subject to interpretation by the local code authorities.

Codes and the Law

It is understandable that people would be confused about the differences between code and law, because they seem to be similar. They are both rules that must be adhered to. In the U.S., these building codes are not United States law, or even state law. This is why there are so many versions of the same code scattered about the U.S. and internationally. In fact, there's no law that says what code must be used. A jurisdiction might even adopt an older version of a code instead of the latest revision.

Code might not be law, but the consequences of ignoring code could result in legal action, particularly if people or property is damaged as a result. Quite simply, you must follow code to get sign-off approval by the building inspectors for the legal right to occupy the building. Occupying a building without the appropriate permits is a violation of law. This is how it works in the U.S. If you are planning to build in another country, make sure you find out how it works there, because other rules (or no rules) could apply.

So, what if you happen to be building in an area where the code restrictions are lax? Maybe you aren't required to meet certain codes such as NFPA 75. Leaving out those expensive fire doors would be a lot cheaper. However, your company might decide that, to create a data center that is safe for employees and equipment, you should build to standards beyond what the local codes require.

Who Can Help?

It is unrealistic to expect data center designers to know all the codes, along with their numerous permutations and interpretations. But designers should know which codes will be used. Again, designers are not working in a vacuum, but have many talented and knowledgeable people on their team, including outside contract professionals. Project management firms, architects, structural, HVAC, and electrical engineers are usually familiar with what code is used in that area and how to work with the local code officials and inspectors.

But how do you really know that these people will give you accurate information? Data center designers should know something about the codes and which codes will be used for their data center. Unfortunately, sometimes sections of these codes can be used to make "black hole" explanations for why things cannot be done or must be done more expensively. It would seem that working with reputable and ethical building professionals, the black hole problem should not occur. However, it could be a policy of a contract firm to interpret code in their favor, adding time and cost to a project. The data center designer should, at the very least, know to question the code and ask for specifics. Which code? Which section of the code? What, exactly, does it specify? Why is it interpreted that way? Armed with a few simple questions, you show that you are not willing to be taken advantage of, you might save the company a pile of money, and it will help you decide on the outside firms with whom you want to develop honest working relationships.

Construction Criteria

A data center requires more precise control over temperature, relative humidity, airflow, electrical capacity and reliability, and contaminants than a typical office environment, and these criteria must be considered throughout the design and construction process. Construction projects are expensive and the construction of controlled data center areas is more expensive than most projects. Despite the pressure of deadlines and to keep within budget, it is important to avoid cutting corners or settling for inferior workmanship even if it will meet code.

A key point here is to design toward your criteria (RLUs, power, HVAC, etc.) for the data center. If your budget will not allow you to implement the results of this design, redefine the criteria and/or scope of the data center.

The following should be kept in mind when planning the construction details.

Construction Materials

All building materials should be chosen with concern for cleanliness and moisture retention. Choose materials that won't shed particulate matter or deteriorate. Close attention should be given to materials for the areas of direct airflow and foot traffic, and to materials that require repeated movement in the normal operations of the room. Certain materials that might shed particulate should be cleaned and treated. Ceiling tiles should have a vinyl or foil face to provide a moisture barrier and prevent the tiles from dropping particles when they are moved. All supply plenum surfaces should be constructed of appropriately treated materials, such as encapsulated concrete, or galvanized or painted metals.

Some materials retain moisture, cause rot, and release particulate. Also, water is an excellent conductor of electricity and presents a grounding and shorting concern.

Materials used in a Class 100,000 clean room would be ideal, but would significantly increase the cost.

Construction in an Operational Data Center

Construction projects occurring in an online data center require additional time, planning, and expense, but precautions are essential for uninterrupted operation. Panels and other items should be pre-cut and drilled outside the center to minimize contaminants.

When the work must be done inside the area, it should be done in such a way to contain or arrest contaminants and particulates. Plastic sheeting should be used to isolate the work space from the rest of the controlled area. Portable filter systems can be used to arrest particulates in the air, but these are only effective in localized areas. If the construction includes drilling or sawing, vacuum units equipped with High Efficiency Particulate Air (HEPA) filtration should be used to collect the dust.

Isolating Construction Activity

If access doors must be kept open due to construction traffic, temporary barriers should be built to isolate dust, stabilize air pressure and temperature, and preserve security. Similar barriers might be necessary if the outer walls are breached during expansion of the area perimeter.

Preserving Environmental Integrity

If raised floor tiles must be removed, make sure that there will be adequate subfloor pressure levels for proper air distribution. Also, if the construction will in any way affect the environmental support equipment, make sure the air conditioning and humidification needs of the center are not significantly compromised. In these situations, redundant HVAC units might be necessary.

Pre-Hardware Installation Checklist

The pre-hardware installation checklist should include specific tasks to fully prepare the data center area to accept the data center hardware.

- **Verify that the room is secure.** Any breach between the data center area and outside areas creates a possible security risk. Make sure all windows are replaced with a barrier or blocked. Also, replace or block any chutes, unnecessary ventilator shafts, mail drops, or slots.

- **Verify that the room is sealed.** This involves not only human security, but the assurance that the vapor barrier is sealed to specifications. In the subfloor void, check perimeter gaps around pipes and conduit, cracks in the deck or walls, expansion joints, open ducts, and walls that connect the subfloor void to the ceiling void or to other floors. Above the raised floor space, check holes or cracks in the perimeter walls, and gaps around pipes, ducts, doors, and light fixtures. Above the drop ceiling, check for gaps around pipes, ducts, and conduit. Also, check for breaches around structural beams, inner walls, access doors and ceiling openings to connected attic areas, and roof vents.

- **Clean the room.** A complete cleaning of the area should be done to remove all major construction equipment, materials, and debris. Low-grade industrial vacuums can be used to remove heavy deposits, wallboard dust, sawdust, and dirt.

- **Test power.** Load test the generators, UPS, chillers, and other power infrastructure components. Test any devices or connections necessary to ensure that the data center is ready to start online computer operations.

- **Label everything.** Make sure all outlets and associated current breakers are labeled.

- **Inspect environmental support equipment.** Check for proper installation and functioning of all environmental support equipment, such as HVAC. Put the air conditioners and humidifiers through their cycles by adjusting their set points to test cooling, heating, humidifying, and dehumidifying. Make all necessary adjustments.

- **Filter the room.** During and after construction cleaning, the air conditioners should be run continuously to filter the room air. These units need not be set for cooling, but just running to remove particulate matter from the room. Ideally, 60 percent efficiency filters should be used. Remember to replace these filters before hardware is installed in the area. They will be full of particulate matter that can be redispersed by the subfloor pressure forcing air in a reverse pattern through a unit should one of the air conditioners be turned off.

- **Decontaminate the room.** At this stage, all residual particulate matter must be removed from the area. All room surfaces must be carefully cleaned. Do not use low-grade vacuum equipment as used in the pre-cleaning stage, because these lack the filtration necessary to keep particulate matter from cycling back into the area. Use vacuums equipped with High Efficiency Particulate Arrestance (HEPA) filtration.

- **Stabilize the environment.** Before installing hardware, the temperature levels, relative humidity levels, subfloor and room pressurization, and airborne particulate levels should be monitored and adjusted. These settings will have to be changed once the hardware with its heat load and designed airflow is in place, but setting the environmental controls of the room in advance will give a stable and more easily adjustable environment to work with.

- **Verify all network drops in PODs and network patch cables.** All network cabling should be verified prior to move-in to ensure that it meets its appropriate specifications, and that all ports are correctly labeled. For patch panel cabling, this verification should be done by the network cabling contractor as defined in the contract. Additionally, patch cables that will connect devices to the PODs and to each other should be verified and labeled. When bringing new configurations online, any number of weird little problems can arise, and verification takes the network and its cabling out of the potential problem path. Also, it is a way to verify that you have adequate quantities of patch cables in the appropriate lengths needed to bring the systems online.

- **Enable infrastructure servers and outside connectivity.** The data center provides physical services like power and cooling. Machines will also require logical services such as Domain Name Service, NIS, LDAP, backups, etc. These services will be used by all configurations in the data center. These servers should be considered part of the data center infrastructure. Since configurations in the data center will need these services, these servers and their associated services should be in place before bringing production machines online. The same is true for outside connectivity. Since most or all configurations will need to pass data outside the data center, this connectivity should be established prior to bringing production machines online. As with verifying network cabling, this verification will ensure that the logical services are available when bringing new configurations online.

Managing System Configurations

Elizabeth Purcell

Performance Availability Engineering Systems Engineer

Abstract

It goes without saying that computer use has exploded in the last decade. Along with this growth has come a corresponding surge in the numbers of devices, services, and data types in corporate data centers, as well as an increasing shift to the 24×7×365 business environment. Consequently, the modern systems administrator is faced with a seemingly bewildering array of hardware, interconnects, and software.

With the intense focus on building out infrastructures, the techniques of cost-effectively managing the increasingly diverse and complex hardware and software solutions often fall by the wayside. Configuration management holds out the promise of making sense of the rats' nest of systems, cabling, software, and patches with a minimum of human effort.

This paper attempts to illustrate some of the issues surrounding the use of configuration management techniques.

Introduction

In the world of systems management, it seems that there is always something that needs to be done. An important aspect of systems management is managing the system configurations. Managing the configuration includes managing the version and revision levels of system and application software, the types and versions of systems and adapters, the networks that the system is attached to, and the storage subsystems and their attachment mechanism, and all software, hardware, and firmware patches for all of the above. While this can seem to be a daunting task, particularly in large, fast-growing, complex environments, the configuration can be managed.

While working with my project, a complex testing environment for investigating integrated systems performance, manageability, and usability, it became clear that the management of the configurations was crucial. Because the project requires many different configurations which change rapidly and may need to be restored quickly, detailed documentation to facilitate rapidly recreating the many possible configurations was mandatory, so the project would not end up being a can of worms and impossible to use effectively.

Managing of a large number of complex systems can be a difficult process. There are so many different hardware and software configurations that are possible, and sometimes it seems that just when you think that you have it right, there are some new requirements that require the configurations to change. Because of all the configuration possibilities and the seemingly constant changes, it's important to manage the configurations carefully. In a data center that is not organized, constant changes could spell near disaster. If a system administrator decides to browse the web, run unauthorized software, and download and listen to music via your important database server, it impacts both the integrity, performance, and manageability of the system. It is important to use the methods and tools that are available to manage the configurations of the systems.

In the Beginning...

It's easier to start out right then to try to retool later. While this is true for most things, it is certainly true for managing the configurations of systems. The more configuration control that has been placed over the system from the beginning, the better the results will be moving forward. Everything from color standardization on cables and labels, the placement of the equipment in the data center, system naming conventions, system installation, and patch maintenance is important.

Correct placement of the equipment in the data center is important, so that the systems do not need to be moved later. If possible, think about the future growth that will be required. Because human interactions with equipment can cause issues like cables to "fall off," the wrong disks to be replaced, the wrong system to be upgraded, it is good to minimize human interactions. In general, the less human contact that the equipment has, the better off it is.

The data center environment should be planned for simplicity and convenience. Is the equipment accessible to what it needs to be accessible to? Are the systems expected to need more storage, and if so, is there room for it? Think about the long term.

Naming conventions become important so the correct system can be quickly identified and found. This is important so that systems are not mistaken for each other and the wrong peripherals or cables are added or removed.

Whenever possible, plan. The old saying of hope for the best but plan for the worst is valid here. In cases where you inherit systems that were never under configuration management, it is possible to get this fixed, but it can be painful to uptime constraints and time consuming for the system administrators.

Systems need to properly labeled so that the systems con be identified quickly and correctly. At minimum, it is important that both the front and the back of the system is labeled. Selecting colors for the labels for similar system types can also be helpful for identification.

Cabling

Color coded network cables have been used in the data center for a long time now. The colors make it easier to identify and locate configurations, as well as assist in quickly resolving simple problems. For example, a blue cable may indicate a connection to a maintenance network while a red cable may indicate a connection to the network service provider and be one of the main connections to the internet. But what happens when you run out of the particular color cable that you need at 2 AM? What do you do about fiber cables that aren't as simple to get in a variety of colors?

An alternative to the use of color coded cables is the use of color cable ties. The cable ties can be used either to adhere the labels to the cable, or it can simply be attached to the ends. The various colors of the cable ties help to identify the type (and use) of the cable, just like the color coded cables, and it seems to work surprisingly well. An added benefit is that it is possible to stock a huge amount of various colors of cable ties in a very small amount of space, especially when compared to the space needed and additional planning necessary to stock color cables.

If you have to stock five different length network cables in eight different colors, you'd need 40 sets of cables stocked and available at any time. With the color cable ties you'd need only five sets of cables and eight bags of cable ties.

Cable labeling should not be ignored. A cable should never be installed that isn't labeled on both ends. This is true for network, FCAL, SCSI and even many power cables. While this seems obvious, it is surprising how many shops don't do this. Tracing cables in the middle of the night in the midst of a crisis is not fun!

Cables for storage devices should also be labeled. It should be readily apparent where each cable on the system is supposed to be in the event the cable is removed and is replaced later.

A labeling scheme should be developed that incorporates the most important details. An example of the types of information to include on a network cable label would be the port number on a switch, the switch in use, the port on the server, and the size of the subnet. Information to include on a storage cable would the server attachment device information and the storage device, and the storage device's attachment device information.

Cables should always be secured so that they do not end up resembling a huge pile of spaghetti. If the cables are neatly secured in bundles, there is a much greater opportunity that the cable can be identified quickly and simply.

Velcro makes a very functional tie wrap, especially when working with cables in racks. Because it is easy of use for both securing and removing cables, it is quite nice for large cable bundles.

System Installation

All system administrators have their favorite way to install systems, and if you get ten system administrators together in a room, there is a good chance that they will disagree on some aspect of what the best setup is. This can be called the "Rule of Ten Systems Administrators." For manageability, it is important that all of the systems of the same type and function be installed in the same reproducible method. Additionally, the less human intervention that is necessary, the better: as the "Rule of Ten Systems Administrators" says, many options are possible, and everyone has their own ideas as to what is "right."

Automation is the key to manageability. It makes installation faster in the long run and less time consuming for administrators. So, all in all, the more automation, the better for managing the configuration.

To make it simpler and even manageable, it is important to be organize the configurations by function and system type. That is, all of the like systems with the same functions will be installed with the same installation process. This has several advantages. First, you know what is on the system so changes for tuning, etc. and be handled easily. and if the system has to be reproduced quickly, just reinstall it. It is important to manage the configurations of each type of system in the enterprise.

Solaris JumpStart Software

It's important that the system get a good start in life. It's initial installation should be as good and complete as it can possibly be. The Solaris™ Operating Environment contains some nice tools to accomplish this. One of the commonly tools is the Solaris JumpStart™ software.

Solaris JumpStart software is a powerful installation tool for systems that will be running the Solaris Operating Environment. Using a Solaris JumpStart server can help reach the goal of total hands-off installation.

Using the "JASS" toolkit, written by Alex Noordergraf and Glen Brunette and available as Sun Blueprint™, http://www.sun.com/blueprints/, as a basic architecture layout and software setup, and adding additional similar scripts, a hands-off installation server can be built that can be expanded to include the installation of many of the tools and applications required for the systems.

Some of the issues encountered along the way to standardization can be patches, storage firmware, and software application versions.

The Solaris JumpStart server is an important aspect of controlling the system configurations. The Solaris JumpStart server should be secure and protected against break-ins because if it is compromised, the files that will be installed onto the systems could be compromised and installed directly into your environment.

Source Control on the Solaris JumpStart Server

Using Solaris JumpStart, Solaris Operating Environment installations can be duplicated quickly. However, what happens if someone decided to incorrectly change the configurations and not tell anyone?

What if the scripts that are being used were modified and you want to go back to a previous configuration? Source control can help will help in this situation.

The Solaris JumpStart server should be under source control. Source control will be able to let you know the history of the files. It will let you know when it was modified, who modified it and when. In large data center environments with many system administrators, this is important because there could be many people with the access to write files. There are several source code control systems available, such as RCS, CVS, and SCCS. SCCS is included in the Solaris Operating Environment and is relatively easy to use.

Using Makefiles, make and a source control software can help automate generation and validation of the install scripts and setup. Because the install server can get quite complicated, the automation of the make files can help maintain order and ease of use.

Packages

How do you know what software and utilities are on your system? How do you know what version is in use?

Use of the packaging facility in Solaris Operating Environment is a great way to add software to the system. Rather then browsing through directories and comparing binaries, pkginfo could be used to inspect the versions of custom software added to the systems. With the use of packages, it is not only simple to see what software is on the system, but what version is on the system, Also, upgrades are simplified. Packaging software is right up there with labeling cables—it really is a must.

The functionality to build packages is built into Solaris Operating Environment. Using the pkgmk and pkgproto commands, packages can be made relatively quickly and easily.

Before packages are built, care should be taken to decide where the code will go on the system. If care isn't taken, the software could end up all over the system. Some people like /usr/local; others insist that /opt as the best location. Probably the most important thing is to decide where your shop will be putting it's software and always do it the way that was decided to. Make exceptions to this rule minimal.

Packages added with pkgadd can be removed using pkgrm. Using the optional preinstall, postinstall, preremove and postremove scripts can be used to further customize the installation and removal processes.

Packages should be made with meaningful names and versions. If the package is named something like tmp1, it may be of little use when trying to determine what it is, but if the package contains the software name and version number, it becomes much more useful and efficient to determine what it contains. It is this information, the names, versions, and creation dates that will help when trying to determine what's on the system.

Packages should be built so that they work well with Solaris JumpStart server. The packages should be created so that they can be deployed in a "hands-off" environment.

Unfortunately, not every third party software is in package format. Personally, I find this to be a bug.

Software Patches

New patches always seem to be coming out. While it is very important to apply these patches, it is also important to be aware of the patch levels on all of the systems that you are trying to manage.

Patches should initially be installed during the at Solaris Operating Environment installation. By doing this, all systems will be at the same level.

Maintenance of the patch levels should be done at regular intervals, if possible. All of the like systems (same application/function) should be done at the same time, if possible. Of course, patches should be tested and then deployed in a staging environment before being put onto production systems.

While it is not always possible, try to keep all of the systems of a like function and type at the same patch level.

Firmware and Storage Patches

Systems do not always arrive at the current OpenBoot™ architecture and FCode (for server I/O boards) level. In order to maintain consistency, be sure to check their levels and make certain that they are consistent with other systems of the like type and function before moving the systems into production.

If an upgrade is necessary, it is usually done via patches. There will be directions that will explain the process to follow. As usual, when adding patches, test before upgrading.

Storage Area Networks

Storage Area Networks (SANs) are coming to many data centers. The storage area network adds some additional complexity not only because it is yet another network to manage, but because it adds additional ways the storage can be configured. Using SAN switches, the storage can be configured in different ways.

The SanSurfer™ GUI is used to configure the Sun StorEdge™ network FC switch. The switch is shipped on a default 10.0.0 network. Due to an Arp timeout issue with some network switches, the switch will not always rarp the new address, so it can become necessary to configure it for the first time on a 10.0.0 network.

In order to manage the Sun StorEdge network FC switch, it is important to understand the configuration files that the switch uses to save the configuration information. The switch's NVRAM contains all of the switches configuration information. This configuration information is saved when the changes are made to the configuration and applied to NVRAM.

The Fabric Archive File (`*.cfg`) contains all the configurable information in a switch: its stage type, chassis and fabric IDs, port modes, IP address, other network configuration information, and all of the zoning information. While this file can be used to replace a switch, it should not used to clone switch configurations due to possible issues that could cause failures like mismatches with fabric IDs, duplicated IP addresses and duplicate chassis IDs.

The Zoning Template File (`*.tpl` and `*.tp2`) contains the zoning information for the fabric. It contains the switches WWNs and port counts. This files helps each zone know the ports and nodes that are configured in it.

The Fabric File (`*.fab`) contains the information shown on the Fabric Display like the IP address, fabric name, and polling information.

List of Things to Remember

I have found, during my work with massively complex system environments, that there are a few top issues that can affect configuration management. Here are some of them:

- Set the explicit disk to use when installing via JumpStart server.
- Check for all patches!
- Read all of the release notes.

- May need to access to a 10.0.0 network for the Sun StorEdge network FC switch's initial configuration.

- When using Fibre channel: be aware of hard address vs. boxid vs. target id.

- When using the Sun StorEdge network FC switch, do not forget to "apply" the changes that were made, as necessary.

- Set port types on SAN switches before making zones.

- Use ports 1, 4, 8 .. to connect to Servers, if possible, for better performance under some conditions.

- Be sure to check the `/etc/system` file. Do not blindly roll things forward, e.g. priority paging.

Conclusions

Simplicity and automation are important keys to configuration management. While the configurations are getting more and more complicated these days with the myriad of hardware and software that are needed, keeping the configuration management organized is key. The simpler the process and the less human intervention that needs to be done results in better configuration management.

Bibliography and References

Many of the books, software, papers, or other materials referred to throughout this book can be ordered by mail or downloaded from the originating organization. The following sections give contact information for most of these organizations and the titles of the referenced materials. This information and other reference materials can also be found at
`http://www.sun.com/blueprints/tools/dcdesign-tools.html`.

Books

The following books are referenced within the chapters of this book:

Capacity Planning for Internet Services. Adrian Cockcroft, Bill Walker. Sun BluePrints, Sun Microsystems Press (A Prentice Hall Title), 2001.

Resource Management. Richard McDougall, Adrian Cockcroft, Evert Hoogendoorn, Enrique Vargas, Tom Bialaski. Sun BluePrints, Sun Microsystems Press (A Prentice Hall Title), 1999.

Sun Performance and Tuning (Second Edition). Adrian Cockcroft, Richard Pettit. Sun Microsystems Press (A Prentice Hall Title), 1998.

Publications

The following documents are referenced within the chapters of this book:

ASHRAE Applications: Chapter 15, "Clean Spaces."

ASHRAE Applications: Chapter 16, "Data Processing System Areas."

ASHRAE Journal. "Filtration and Indoor Air Quality: A Practical Approach."

ASHRAE 127-1988, "Method of Testing for Rating Computer and Data Processing Room Unitary Air-Conditioners."

ASTM F 50-92, "Standard Practice for Continuous Sizing and Counting of Airborne Particles in Dust-Controlled Areas and Clean Rooms Using Instruments Capable of Detecting Single Sub-Micrometer and Larger Particles."

ANSI/EOS/ESD - S6.1-1991, "EOS/ESD Association Standard for Protection of Electrostatic Discharge Susceptible Items, Grounding—Recommended Practice."

Federal Standard 209E (IEST), "Airborne Particulate Cleanliness Classes in Cleanrooms and Clean Zones."

FIPS PUB 94, "Guidelines on Electrical Power for ADP Installations." (From the U.S. Department of Commerce, National Bureau of Standards.)

IEC 1000-4-5, "Surge Immunity Requirements."

IEEE STD 1100-1992, "Powering and Grounding Sensitive Electronic Equipment."

ISA-71.04-1985, "Environmental Conditions for Process Measurement and Control Systems: Airborne Contaminants."

NFPA 70, "National Electrical Code."

WES 45-01-10, "The Effect of the Environment on Computer Operations."

Organizations

Following are organizations and companies that have performed testing and written the definitive standards for specific subjects that relate to data center design and construction.

American Society of Heating, Refrigeration, and Air-Conditioning Engineers, Inc. (ASHRAE)
Web site: http://www.ashrae.org
Address: 1791 Tullie Circle, N.E., Atlanta, GA 30329, USA
Toll Free: (800) 527-4723 (U.S. and Canada only)
Phone: (404) 636-8400
Fax: (404) 321-5478

American Society for Testing and Materials (ASTM)
Web site: http://www.astm.org
Address: 100 Barr Harbor Drive, West Conshohocken, PA, USA 19428-2959, USA
Phone: (610) 832-9585
Fax: (610) 832-9555

Electrostatic Discharge Association, Inc. (EOS/ESD)
Web site: http://www.esda.org
Email: eosesd@aol.com
Address: 7900 Turin Road, Building 3, Suite 2, Rome, NY 13440-2069, USA
Phone: (315) 339-6937
Fax: (315) 339-6793

Institute of Electrical and Electronics Engineers, Inc. (IEEE)
Web site: http://www.ieee.org

Instrumentations, Systems, and Automation Society (ISA)
Web site: http://www.isa.org
Address: 67 Alexander Drive, Research Triangle Park, NC, 27709, USA
Phone: (919) 549-8411
Fax: (919) 549-8288

International Electrotechnical Commission (IEC)
Web site: http://www.iec.ch
Address: 3, rue de Varembé, P.O. Box 131, CH - 1211 GENEVA 20, Switzerland
Phone: +41 22 919 02 11
Fax: +41 22 919 03 00

Institute of Environmental Sciences and Technology (IEST)
Web site: http://www.iest.org
Address: 940 East Northwest Highway, Mount Prospect, IL 60056,USA
Phone: (847) 255-1561
Fax: (847) 255-1699

National Fire Prevention Association (NFPA)
Web site: http://www.nfpa.org
Email: custserv@nfpa.org
Address: 1 Batterymarch Park, P.O. Box 9101, Quincy, MA 02269-9101
Main Switchboard: (617) 770-3000
Fax: (617) 770-0700

U.S. Department of Commerce, National Bureau of Standards
Web site: http://www.doc.gov

Worldwide Environmental Services (WES)
Web site: http://www.wes.net
Mailing Address: P.O. Box 1541, Blue Bell, PA, 19422-0440, USA
Phone: (215) 619-0980
Fax: (215) 619-0990
Toll Free in USA: 1-800-843-5307

Building Officials and Code Administrators International, Inc. (BOCA)
Web site: www.bocai.org
Email: info@bocai.org
Address: 4051 West Flossmoor Road, Country Club Hills, IL 60478
Phone: (800) 214-4321 or (708) 799-2300
Fax: (800) 214-7167

International Code Council (ICC)
Web site: www.intlcode.org
Email: staff@intlcode.org
Address: 5203 Leesburg Pike, Suite 708, Falls Church, VA 22041
Phone: (703) 931-4533
Fax: (703) 379-1546

International Conference of Building Officials (ICBO)
Web site: www.icbo.org
Email: info@icbo.org
Address: 5360 Workman Mill Road, Whittier, CA 90601-2298
Phone (for ordering): (800) 284-4406 or (562) 699-0541
Fax: (310) 692-3858

National Conference of States on Building Codes and Standards (NCSBC)
Web site: www.ncsbcs.org
Email: jmoreschi@ncsbcs.org
Address: 505 Huntmar Park Drive, Suite 210, Herndon, VA 20170
Phone: (703) 437-0100; Fax: (703) 481-3596

North American Insulation Manufacturers Association (NAIMA)
Web site: www.naima.org
Email: insulation@naima.org
Address: 44 Canal Center Plaza, Suite 310, Alexandria, VA 22314
Phone: (703) 684-0084; Fax: (703) 684-0427

Southern Building Code Congress International, Inc. (SBCCI)
Web site: www.sbcci.org
Email: info@sbcci.org
Address: 900 Montclair Road, Birmingham, AL 35213-1206
Phone: (205) 591-1853, Fax: (205) 591-0775

Software

AutoCAD by AutoDesk
http://www.autodesk.com

Flovent by Flomerics
http://www.flometrics.com

Aperture
http://www.aperture.com

Quote Acknowledgments

Quote from Chapter 2 is from "The Adventure of the Beryl Coronet" by Sir Arthur Conan Doyle.

Quote from Chapter 3 is from "A Scandal In Bohemia" by Sir Arthur Conan Doyle.

Quote from Chapter 5 is from "The Adventure of the Copper Beeches" by Sir Arthur Conan Doyle.

Quote from Chapter 6 is from *Henry IV, Part II* by William Shakespeare.

Quote from Chapter 7 is from the song "Gimme Gimme Shock Treatment" by The Ramones, from the album *Ramones Leave Home*, original recording by Tony Bongiovi and T. Erdelyi, 2001. Reissue Warner Bros. Records Inc. and Rhino Entertainment Company.

Quote from Chapter 8 is from the song "Hot You're Cool" by General Public, from the album *All The Rage*. Song by General Public and Published by In General Ltd. / I.R.S. Music Inc.

Quote from Chapter 10 is from the song "Inside Outside" from album *Inside Outside 7*" by Classix Nouveaux. Song by Sal Solo/Nik Sweeney and produced by Solo/Sweeney. Copyright of the sound recording is Owned by EMI Records Ltd.

Quote from Chapter 11 is from the song "London Calling" from the album *London Calling* by The Clash. Song by J. Strummer and M. Jones. Produced by Guy Stevens Published by Epic Records/CBS Inc.

Quote from Chapter 12 is by Lenny Henry who plays Gareth Blackstock in *Chef!* Written by Peter Tilbury. Directed by John Birkin. Produced by Charlie Hanson. An APC Production for BBC in association with Crucial Films.

Quote from Chapter 13 is by Nigel Hawthorne who plays Sir Humphrey in *Yes, Minister*. Written by Antony Jay and Jonathan Lynn. Produced by Stuart Allen for BBC.

Glossary

amps	A steady state current that is created by applying one volt across one ohm of resistance. To calculate amps, divide watts by volts. Watts Volts = Amps.
basic thermal unit or British thermal unit (BTU)	This could be called either, depending on whom you ask. It is a measure of the amount of thermal energy required to raise by one degree 16 oz of water. To calculate BTUs per hour, multiply watts by 3.42. Watts $\times$ 3.42 = BTUs per hour.
Bolognese sauce	A tomato/meat sauce for use on pasta. Al's Mom's Recipe for "Quick Sauce" a.k.a. Bolognese sauce, printed with permission of Fran Mello. Ingredients: 1 lb ground meat (usually beef but could be chicken) 2 Tbs olive oil 2-3 cloves of fresh crushed garlic 2-3 crushed tomatoes or about a cup and half of tomato puree. Oregano, salt, and pepper to taste. Braise the meat in the olive oil and garlic. Add the crushed tomatoes or tomato puree. Cook this mixture over medium heat for as long as it takes your pasta to cook, once the water is at the boil. Add the oregano, salt, and pepper to taste.
electrostatic discharge (ESD)	The static shock you might give by walking across carpet with wool socks and touching a metal door knob. While a fairly minor annoyance in most areas of life, ESD can wreak havoc with electronic components, causing equipment failure.
heating, ventilation, and air-conditioning (HVAC)	This generally refers to the air conditioning system in the data center.
plenum	From the Latin plenus. A area of a room filled with air such as the space between the subfloor and the raised floor, used to move cooling air to racks on the floor.

point of distribution (POD)	A rack containing network switches, terminal servers, and network cable patch ports.
power distribution unit (PDU)	An electrical distribution box fed by a 100 Amp three-phase Hubble connector. This box contains power outlets and circuit breakers.
psychrometry	The study of moist air and the changes in its conditions.
quality of service (QoS)	The delivery of a specific amount of network bandwidth. Defined for Ethernet in the IEEE 802.3q specification.
rack location units (RLU)	A set of specifications (power, cooling, physical space, network connectivity, rack weight, and logical capacity) used to define a rack of computer equipment and serve as a measure for determining data center requirements.
relative humidity (RH)	The ratio of how much moisture is in a volume of air, relative to how much moisture the same volume of air can hold. If you have a 50 percent relative humidity, the air could hold twice as much moisture as it is currently holding.
reverse engineering	The ability to take a completed system and work backwards to figure out how it was constructed.
U	A unit of measure for the sizing of network equipment. 1U is equal to 1.75 inches (44.45 mm) in height. A typical 7-foot rack contains about 6.5 feet of usable rack space, or 45 U tall (1.75 in. $\times$ 45 = 78.75 in.). When you are calculating how many devices you can fit in a rack, you need to know the number of Us of each device.
uninterruptible power supply (UPS)	A very large battery capable of sustaining power load for a given amount of time. If power is fed to it continuously, it can also serve as a power filter.
virtual private network (VPN)	To send data in a secure fashion over a unsecured network through encryption.
volts	The difference in electrical potential between two points on a conductive wire carrying a one ampere constant current. To calculate volts, divide watts by amps. (Watts Amps = Volts)
wide area network (WAN)	Special purpose networks to provide connectivity to multiple locations in different areas.
watts	Equal to 1/746 horsepower. To calculate watts, multiply volts times amps. (Volts $\times$ Amps = Watts)

Index